chinatown
sweet sour spicy salty

Thank you

For most of us, our culinary experience in suburban Australia in the 70s was a limited one.
Fortunately for me, our neighbours were Chinese.
By passing all sorts of Cantonese delights over our backyard fence and taking me on excursions to
Sydney's dynamic Chinatown, they unwittingly ignited and inspired my enthusiasm for Chinese food and
my love of Chinatowns and ethnic food markets all over the world.
Thank you to Isabel Chung for all your wonderful food.

Published by Murdoch Books Pty Limited.

Murdoch Books Australia
Pier 8/9, 23 Hickson Road, Millers Point NSW 2000
Phone: +61 (0)2 8220 2000 Fax: +61 (0)2 8220 2558

Murdoch Books UK Limited
Erico House, 6th Floor North, 93–99 Upper Richmond Road
Putney, London SW15 2TG
Phone: +44 (0)20 8785 5995 Fax: +44 (0)20 8785 5985

Chief executive: Juliet Rogers
Publisher: Kay Scarlett

Design manager: Vivien Valk
Design concept: Marylouise Brammer
Designer: Tracy Loughlin
Project manager: Zoë Harpham
Editor: Kim Rowney
Food preparation: Ross Dobson
Photographer: Mikkel Vang
Stylist: Christine Rudolph
Production: Monika Vidovic
Photographer's assistant: Andrew Wilson
Stylist's assistant: Nina Ross

National Library of Australia Cataloguing-in-Publication Data
Dobson, Ross, 1965– .
Chinatown: sweet, sour, spicy, salty.
Includes index.
ISBN 1 74045 397 2.
1. Cookery, Chinese. I. Title
641.5951

Printed by Midas Printing (ASIA) Ltd. PRINTED IN CHINA.
First published 2005.

IMPORTANT: Those who might be at risk from the effects of salmonella poisoning (the elderly, pregnant women, young children and those suffering from immune deficiency diseases) should consult their doctor with any concerns about eating raw eggs.

CONVERSION GUIDE: You may find cooking times vary depending on the oven you are using. For fan-forced ovens, as a general rule, set the oven temperature to 20°C (35°F) lower than indicated in the recipe. We have used 20 ml (4 teaspoon) tablespoon measures. If you are using a 15 ml (3 teaspoon) tablespoon, for most recipes the difference will not be noticeable. However, for recipes using baking powder, gelatine, bicarbonate of soda (baking soda) or small amounts of cornflour (cornstarch), add an extra teaspoon for each tablespoon specified.

The Publisher thanks Bamboo Home, Chefland, Dean and DeLuca, Mud Australia, Papaya, The Essential Ingredient and The Orient Express for their assistance with the photography for this book.

chinatown
sweet sour spicy salty

ross dobson

photography by Mikkel Vang
styling by Christine Rudolph

MURDOCH BOOKS

contents

lotus flowers and liquorice root   6

salt   10

spice   62

sour   112

sweet   142

basic recipes   187

glossary   188

index   190

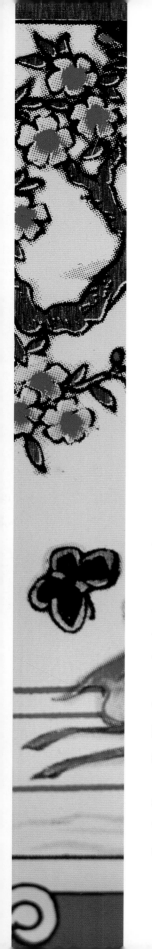

lotus flowers and liquorice root

In most cities you will find a Chinatown: a buzzing, electric enclave of neon-bright lights, alive with exotic colours, smells and flavours. Colourful paper parasols, fire-red lanterns, dragons and fire crackers wait to explode into a celebration of colour and movement.

Noodle houses, dim sum houses and mahjong rooms compete with the sound of the wok charn clanging as it hits the wok. Metal on hot metal, breathing heat and life into food.

The wonderful flavours of Chinatown.
The crazy, chaotic buzz of a Chinatown market.
The intoxicating and seductive smells of barbecue and spice.

To many of us the ingredients sold here will look, smell and sound irresistibly exotic: sichuan peppercorns, dried tangerine peel, rock sugar, lotus flowers and liquorice root.

Chinatown will explore some of these magical ingredients, combining them with fresh produce to create a simple and flavour-explosive cuisine. A cuisine with celestial flavours. The flavours of Chinatown.

Salt is of the earth. Salt is the humble and ancient soya bean, as old as culinary time itself. It is soy sauce. Pure, organic salt preserves and balances flavour.

Spice is explosive and fiery. Chillies. Fresh and dried, large and small, hanging like fireworks on a fuse. Spice is intoxicating and complex. The heady aromas of a Chinatown spice market, sending our senses into a spin.

Sour is zest and tang. A yin and yang balance. Vinegars, clear and crisp or rich and dark, resonating a malty depth of flavour. Sour is citrus fresh and excites the taste buds.

Sweet is sugar and honey. Seductive and enticing. The fruits of prosperity and good fortune. Warmth and laughter.

To paraphrase a Chinese poet from ancient times:

Good cooking does not depend on whether the dish is small,
expensive or economical.
Salty dishes should come first…
If you suspect your dinner guests
have eaten their fill,
you must stir them into action with spice,
you must enliven them with sour and sweet!

salt

The process of pouring hot, smoking oil over food is very Cantonese. This technique is like alchemy, here producing a silky-smooth, mildly salty sauce that lightly coats the prawns when they are dipped.

steamed prawns with garlic soy

2 tablespoons light soy sauce
2 garlic cloves, crushed
¼ teaspoon caster (superfine) sugar
2 teaspoons peanut oil
24 raw small to medium prawns (shrimp)

Serves 4 as a starter

Put the soy sauce, garlic and sugar in a small heatproof bowl. Heat the oil in a saucepan over high heat. When the oil reaches smoking point, pour the hot oil over the soy sauce mixture and stir to combine. Set aside to allow the flavours to develop.

Meanwhile, bring a wok or large saucepan of water to the boil. Put some baking paper in the bottom of a large bamboo steamer. Prick holes in the paper with a fork or skewer and arrange the prawns in a single layer. Cover with the lid and steam over boiling water for 6–7 minutes, or until the prawns turn pink. Remove and place on a serving platter. Peel the prawns at the table and serve with the garlic and soy dip.

These delicious rolls are filled with crisp, fresh Chinatown market ingredients.

egg rolls with vegetables and coriander

90 g (3¼ oz/¾ cup) plain (all-purpose) flour
2 eggs, lightly beaten
canola or vegetable oil, for frying
½ carrot, cut into thin 4 cm (1½ in) lengths
1 celery stalk, cut into thin 4 cm (1½ in) lengths
1 large handful bean sprouts
2 spring onions (scallions), shredded into 4 cm (1½ in) lengths
1 small handful coriander (cilantro) sprigs, cut into 4 cm (1½ in) lengths
185 ml (6 fl oz/¾ cup) chicken stock (page 187)
1 tablespoon light soy sauce
1 tablespoon oyster sauce
2 teaspoons cornflour (cornstarch)

Serves 4 as a starter

Put the flour in a food processor with a pinch of salt. With the motor running, add the eggs and 250 ml (9 fl oz/1 cup) water and process for 1 minute to form a smooth batter. Brush a 22 cm (8½ in) non-stick frying pan with a little oil and place over medium heat. Pour in 100 ml (3½ fl oz) of the batter and swirl it around to coat the bottom of the pan. Cook for 2–3 minutes, or until the top has just set, then slide onto a plate. Repeat with the remaining batter (reserving 2 teaspoons of batter) to make three more pancakes.

Bring a saucepan of water to the boil, add the carrot, celery and bean sprouts and cook for 1 minute. Drain well and, when cool, put into a bowl with the spring onions and coriander. Put one of the pancakes in front of you. Place a quarter of the vegetable filling in a mound, 2–3 cm (¾–1¼ in) in from the edge closest to you and 3–4 cm (1¼–1½ in) in from the sides. Firmly roll over the edge closest to you to enclose the filling. Bring in the sides and continue rolling, then seal the end with some of the reserved batter. Repeat to make three more rolls.

Pour enough oil into a frying pan to come 1 cm (½ in) up the side of the pan, and heat over medium heat. Add the rolls, seam side down, and cook for 2–3 minutes, then turn and cook the other side for 2–3 minutes, or until golden. Drain on paper towels.

Put the stock, soy sauce, oyster sauce and cornflour in a saucepan and stir until the cornflour has dissolved. Place over high heat and bring to the boil for 1 minute, stirring, until the sauce is smooth and slightly thickened. Arrange the egg rolls on a plate and pour over the sauce.

This soup has some of the best things Chinatown has to offer, including wonderful char siu (barbecued pork), fresh egg noodles and ginger. More impressively, it can be prepared in under 10 minutes.

ginger broth with barbecued pork

1.25 litres (44 fl oz/5 cups) chicken stock (ready-made or see page 187)
6 thin slices fresh ginger
1 tablespoon light soy sauce
200 g (7 oz) Chinese broccoli (gai larn), cut into 3 cm (1¼ in) slices
200 g (7 oz) fresh thin egg noodles
100 g (3½ oz) Chinese barbecued pork (char siu), thinly sliced
2 spring onions (scallions), thinly sliced on the diagonal
1 teaspoon sesame oil

Serves 6 as a starter

Bring a large saucepan of water to the boil. Put the stock, ginger and soy sauce in another saucepan and bring to the boil, then add the Chinese broccoli, reduce the heat and simmer for 5 minutes.

Meanwhile, add the noodles to the boiling water. When the water returns to the boil, the noodles are ready. Drain and divide the noodles among six small serving bowls. Ladle the ginger broth and Chinese broccoli over the noodles and arrange the pork slices on top. Sprinkle with the spring onions and drizzle with the sesame oil.

Carpaccio is an Italian classic, but here it is given a Chinatown twist with the addition of soy sauce and sesame oil. Freezing the beef first enables it to be sliced wafer thin.

chinatown carpaccio

200 g (7 oz) beef fillet, trimmed
2 tablespoons light soy sauce
2 teaspoons caster (superfine) sugar
¼ teaspoon sesame oil
4 Chinese cabbage (wong bok) leaves, core discarded, very thinly sliced
1 lemon, cut into wedges

Serves 4 as a starter

Put the beef in the freezer for a few hours, or until firm. Using a sharp knife, slice the beef very thinly across the grain and arrange the slices on a serving platter. Cover with plastic wrap and allow the beef to come to room temperature.

Combine the soy sauce, sugar and sesame oil in a small saucepan over medium heat. When the mixture comes to the boil, remove from the heat immediately and stir to dissolve the sugar. Allow to cool.

To serve, scatter the sliced cabbage over the beef and drizzle over the sauce. Serve with a lemon wedge to squeeze over just before eating.

Fresh ginger may very well be the embodiment of Chinese food. Here we have ginger and spring onion, the quintessential yin–yang balance, complementing the sweet flesh of the prawns.

prawns with ginger and spring onion

12 raw large prawns (shrimp)
1 tablespoon shaoxing rice wine
5–6 spring onions (scallions), finely chopped
1 tablespoon grated fresh ginger
1 teaspoon light soy sauce
3 tablespoons peanut oil, plus extra for brushing
sea salt flakes, to serve

Serves 4 as a starter

To remove the vein without peeling the prawn, make an incision on the back of the prawn, just behind the head, and another incision just above the tail. Use a toothpick or a pair of kitchen tweezers to slowly pull up and remove the vein from the incision behind the head. On large prawns the vein should come out easily. Put the prawns in a bowl with the rice wine and toss to coat the prawns in the wine. Refrigerate for 30 minutes.

Put the spring onions, ginger and soy sauce in a heatproof bowl. Heat the oil in a small saucepan over high heat. When the oil reaches smoking point, pour the hot oil over the ingredients in the bowl. Stir to combine and set aside to cool.

Preheat a chargrill pan or barbecue to high heat. Lightly brush the prawns with some of the extra oil and cook for 3 minutes each side, or until the prawns turn pink. Arrange on a platter and sprinkle with sea salt. Serve with the spring onion and ginger dipping sauce and provide finger bowls for your guests.

I love cooking ribs. They are an impressive, inexpensive and slightly exotic cut of meat. Here they are coated in a rich garlicky sauce.

garlic spareribs

500 g (1 lb 2 oz) pork spareribs, cut into 4–5 cm (1½–2 in) lengths
185 ml (6 fl oz/¾ cup) chicken stock (page 187)
½ teaspoon caster (superfine) sugar
5 garlic cloves, crushed
1 tablespoon dark soy sauce
1 tablespoon oyster sauce
1 teaspoon sesame oil
1 tablespoon peanut oil

Serves 4 as a starter

Bring a wok or large saucepan of water to the boil. Put some baking paper in the bottom of a large bamboo steamer and prick holes in the paper with a fork or skewer. Cut between each pork rib and put them in the steamer. Cover with the lid and steam over boiling water for 20 minutes.

Combine the stock, sugar, garlic, soy sauce, oyster sauce and sesame oil in a bowl.

Heat a wok over high heat and add the peanut oil, swirling the oil around to coat the wok. When the oil reaches smoking point, add the ribs. Stir-fry the ribs for 2 minutes, turning them over so they cook evenly. Pour in the sauce mixture and bring to the boil. Cook for 5 minutes, stirring occasionally to evenly coat the ribs in the sauce. The ribs are ready when the sauce has almost evaporated and is very dark in colour.

Hint: Pork ribs are sold in a slab, and are sometimes called American-style pork ribs. Ask your butcher to cut the ribs into the desired length, as they are very difficult to cut at home.

Just a small amount of barley in a soup or stew not only thickens it but also imparts a lovely wholesome, nutty flavour. For this soup, be sure to use pearl barley, which has had the husk removed, therefore reducing the cooking time.

barley and vegetable soup

6 small, dried shiitake mushrooms
1 tablespoon vegetable oil
1 small onion, chopped
1 garlic clove, roughly chopped
2 teaspoons grated fresh ginger
1 celery stalk, thinly sliced
1 carrot, cut in half lengthways and thinly sliced
1.5 litres (52 fl oz/6 cups) chicken stock (page 187)
110 g (3¾ oz/½ cup) pearl barley
1 tablespoon light soy sauce
1 teaspoon sesame oil

Serves 6 as a starter, or 4 as a main

Put the dried mushrooms in a bowl, cover with boiling water and soak for 20–30 minutes. Squeeze out the excess liquid from the mushrooms, then remove and discard the stems and thinly slice the caps. Reserve 125 ml (4 fl oz/½ cup) of the soaking liquid.

Heat the vegetable oil in a saucepan over medium heat and cook the onion and garlic for 2 minutes, or until the onion has just softened. Add the ginger, celery and carrot and cook for 1 minute, then add the stock, barley, soy sauce, reserved mushroom soaking liquid and season with black pepper. Bring to the boil, then reduce to a simmer and cook, uncovered, over low heat for 40 minutes, or until the barley is soft and plump, stirring often. Scatter over the mushrooms and serve drizzled with the sesame oil.

This is the Chinatown version of that great Japanese dish, *agedashi tofu*. The traditional method uses dashi, but fish sauce is a more accessible substitute and, although mostly used in Thai cooking, is readily found in Chinatown.

tofu with soy and ginger

300 g (10½ oz) silken firm tofu
2 tablespoons light soy sauce
1 tablespoon fish sauce
2 teaspoons grated fresh ginger
750 ml (26 fl oz/3 cups) canola or vegetable oil
35 g (1¼ oz/¼ cup) tapioca flour
½ teaspoon ground white pepper
2 spring onions (scallions), green part only, thinly sliced on the diagonal

Serves 4 as part of a main

Cut the tofu into 2–3 cm (¾–1¼ in) cubes and carefully put the cubes onto a plate lined with a couple of layers of paper towel. Place a couple more layers of paper towel on top and leave for 20–30 minutes to allow the excess liquid to be absorbed.

Meanwhile, put the soy sauce, fish sauce and ginger in a small saucepan with 200 ml (7 fl oz) water and bring to a gentle simmer for 1 minute to soften the ginger. Remove from the heat.

Heat the oil in a wok over high heat. The oil is hot enough when the surface starts to shimmer. Put the tapioca flour in a bowl and toss half the tofu in the flour, shake off the excess flour, and deep-fry for 1 minute, or until the tofu is lightly golden. Drain on paper towels and repeat with the remaining tofu.

Put the tofu on a serving plate. Quickly reheat the sauce mixture and pour over the tofu. Sprinkle with the white pepper and spring onions.

Egg noodles are among the most wonderful and versatile fresh ingredients that Chinatown has to offer. They are often used in soups, but also work well in this simple stir-fry.

sesame noodles with garlic chives

300 g (10½ oz) fresh thin egg noodles
2 teaspoons sesame oil
2 tablespoons peanut oil
1 garlic clove, roughly chopped
2 teaspoons grated fresh ginger
100 g (3½ oz/1 bunch) garlic chives, cut into 3 cm (1¼ in) lengths
2 large handfuls bean sprouts
2 tablespoons oyster sauce
1 tablespoon dark soy sauce
2 teaspoons sesame seeds, toasted
Chinese chilli sauce, to serve

Serves 4 as part of a main

Bring a large saucepan of water to the boil and add the noodles. Cook for 2 minutes, then drain, rinse and drain again. Spread the noodles out on a clean tea towel and roll up to extract the excess moisture. Put the noodles in a large bowl with the sesame oil and toss to evenly coat the noodles in the oil.

Heat the peanut oil in a wok over high heat, swirling the oil to coat the wok. Add the garlic and ginger and cook for a few seconds. Add the garlic chives and bean sprouts and stir-fry for 1 minute, or until the sprouts just begin to wilt. Add the noodles, stir-fry for 2 minutes, then stir in the oyster sauce and soy sauce. Toss the ingredients around in the wok for a further minute, or until the noodles are evenly coated in the sauce. Sprinkle with the sesame seeds and serve with a generous dollop of chilli sauce.

Potato is a common ingredient in northern Chinese cooking. Here, the potatoes are julienned, stir-fried and then doused with black vinegar and sprinkled with flakes of sea salt.

stir-fried potato with black vinegar

600 g (1 lb 5 oz) large boiling potatoes, such as nicola
3 tablespoons peanut oil
2 tablespoons Chinese black vinegar
1 tablespoon light soy sauce
1 teaspoon sea salt flakes
small coriander (cilantro) leaves, to garnish
½ teaspoon chilli flakes (optional)

Serves 4 as part of a main

Bring a large saucepan of lightly salted water to the boil. Meanwhile, cut the potatoes into 5 mm (¼ in) thick slices, then very finely julienne. Add the potato to the boiling water and cook for 1 minute, using a pair of tongs or long chopsticks to separate the pieces. Drain the potato slices well and lay out to dry for a few hours on a clean tea towel.

Heat a wok over high heat and add the oil, swirling the oil around to coat the wok. Add the potato and stir-fry for 6 minutes, or until golden. Add the vinegar and soy sauce to the wok and season with ½ teaspoon of sea salt. Stir-fry for 2–3 minutes, or until the potato slices darken and any liquid has evaporated. Sprinkle the remaining salt over the top and garnish with coriander and chilli flakes, if using.

In Chinatown you will see a huge variety of dried mushrooms. For this dish, I have used the dried shiitake with smooth, brown caps. Shiitake have an earthy, dusky aroma and plump up beautifully after soaking. The soaking liquid is also added to the dish to give it extra flavour.

shiitake and gai larn stir-fry

8 dried shiitake mushrooms
2 tablespoons oyster sauce
1 tablespoon light soy sauce
1/2 teaspoon caster (superfine) sugar
2 tablespoons peanut oil
2 teaspoons grated fresh ginger
2 garlic cloves, roughly chopped
4 spring onions (scallions), cut into 3 cm (1¼ in) lengths
750 g (1 lb 10 oz/1 bunch) Chinese broccoli (gai larn), cut into
    6 cm (2½ in) lengths

Serves 4 as part of a main

Put the mushrooms in a bowl, cover with boiling water and soak for 20–30 minutes. Squeeze out the excess liquid from the mushrooms, then remove and discard the stems and cut the caps in half. Reserve 60 ml (2 fl oz/¼ cup) of the soaking liquid.

Combine the oyster sauce, soy sauce and sugar in a bowl, stirring to dissolve the sugar.

Heat a wok over high heat and add the oil, swirling the oil around to coat the wok. Add the ginger, garlic and spring onions and stir-fry for 10 seconds. Add the mushrooms and stir-fry for 1 minute, then add the broccoli and stir-fry for 2 minutes. Pour the sauce mixture and the reserved mushroom soaking liquid into the wok, pouring them down the side of the wok. Stir-fry for 1 minute to evenly coat all the ingredients in the sauce.

This is so simple and fresh it deserves the best quality soy sauce. Light soy sauce, as used here and in most stir-fries, is saltier than dark soy, which is thicker, has a malty flavour and used mostly in slow-cooked dishes. Always try to use soy sauce that has been naturally fermented.

prawn, celery and garlic fried rice

3 tablespoons peanut oil
16 raw medium prawns (shrimp), peeled and deveined with tails intact
4 garlic cloves, finely chopped
1 teaspoon grated fresh ginger
2 spring onions (scallions), thinly sliced on the diagonal
2 celery stalks, thinly sliced on the diagonal
550 g (1 lb 4 oz/3 cups) cooked, cooled long-grain rice
2 tablespoons light soy sauce
1 teaspoon ground white pepper
1 teaspoon sesame oil

Serves 4 as part of a main

Heat a wok over high heat and add the peanut oil, swirling the oil around to coat the wok. Add the prawns, garlic, ginger and spring onions and stir-fry for 1 minute, or until the prawns turn pink. Add the celery and stir-fry for 1–2 minutes.

Add the rice and stir-fry for 2 minutes, then add the soy sauce, pouring it down the side of the wok. Sprinkle in the pepper and stir-fry for 1 minute, ensuring the ingredients are evenly coated in the soy sauce. Drizzle with the sesame oil and serve.

Hint: For 550 g (1 lb 4 oz/3 cups) cooked long-grain rice, you will need 200 g (7 oz/1 cup) raw rice. Allow the rice to cool thoroughly before using it.

The silken tofu used in this recipe is, as its name suggests, silky and light—steaming the tofu helps to maintain its silkiness. The creamy texture of the tofu is enhanced by the saltiness of the mushroom and light soy sauces.

silken tofu with soy, chilli and spring onion

300 g (10½ oz) block silken firm tofu
1 teaspoon mushroom soy sauce
1 tablespoon light soy sauce
1 tablespoon shaoxing rice wine
½ teaspoon caster (superfine) sugar
1 small red chilli, thinly sliced on the diagonal
2 spring onions (scallions), thinly sliced on the diagonal
2 tablespoons chopped coriander (cilantro) leaves
2 tablespoons peanut oil
1 teaspoon sesame oil

Serves 4 as part of a main

Carefully tip the block of tofu out of its container and onto a plate lined with a couple of layers of paper towel. Place a couple more layers of paper towel on top and leave for 20–30 minutes to allow the excess liquid to be absorbed.

Bring a wok or saucepan of water to the boil. Cut the drained tofu into six to eight pieces. Put the tofu on a heatproof plate, then put the plate in a bamboo steamer. Combine the mushroom and soy sauces, rice wine and sugar in a bowl and pour over the tofu. Place a lid on the bamboo steamer and steam the tofu over boiling water for 10 minutes. Carefully remove the hot plate from the steamer.

Sprinkle the chilli, spring onions and coriander over the tofu. Heat the peanut and sesame oils in a small saucepan over high heat until the oil reaches smoking point, then pour the hot oil over the tofu. Serve immediately.

Lobster is not cheap, and the last thing you want is a fussy, time-consuming recipe. This one is short and sweet and pays respect to this wonderful ingredient, in a very Chinese way.

salt and chilli lobster

1 raw lobster tail, about 800 g–1 kg (1 lb 12 oz–2 lb 4 oz)
3 tablespoons shaoxing rice wine
½ teaspoon caster (superfine) sugar
2 tablespoons light soy sauce
1 large red chilli, thinly sliced
1 large green chilli, thinly sliced
canola or vegetable oil, for deep-frying
2 tablespoons sea salt flakes
60 g (2¼ oz/½ cup) cornflour (cornstarch)
½ iceberg lettuce, cut into 1 cm (½ in) strips

Serves 4 as a main

To prepare the lobster tail, cut the tail crossways into five or six medallions, leaving the medallions in the shell.

Combine the rice wine and sugar in a large non-metallic bowl and add the lobster medallions, tossing them to coat in the marinade. Refrigerate for about 20 minutes. In a small bowl, combine the soy sauce with half the red and green chillies and set aside.

Half-fill a wok with the oil and place over high heat. The oil is hot enough when the surface starts to shimmer. Add the remaining chilli slices to the oil and cook for 20–30 seconds, then drain on paper towels.

Put the sea salt in a bowl and rub the flakes between your fingers to break up any large pieces. Add the cornflour and stir to combine. Remove the lobster from the marinade and drain. Toss the lobster medallions in the salt and cornflour mixture, shaking off any excess. Lower the lobster into the hot oil and cook for 2 minutes, or until the lobster shell turns red and the flesh is opaque. Remove and drain on paper towels. Arrange the lettuce on a serving plate, top with the lobster and sprinkle over the fried chillies. Serve with the soy dipping sauce on the side.

Explore the exotic varieties of fresh mushrooms available in Chinatown. The mushrooms used here work well in quick stir-fries, but avoid field mushroom varieties as they sweat and darken when cooked.

chinatown mushroom and tofu stir-fry

3 tablespoons chicken stock (page 187)
2 tablespoons oyster sauce
1 tablespoon soy sauce
3 tablespoons peanut oil
200 g (7 oz) firm tofu, cut into 2 cm (¾ in) cubes
3 spring onions (scallions), finely chopped
1 teaspoon grated fresh ginger
1 garlic clove, finely chopped
100 g (3½ oz/1⅓ cups) enoki mushrooms, trimmed
150 g (5½ oz/2 cups) oyster mushrooms, large ones cut in half
100 g (3½ oz/2 cups) small shiitake mushrooms, stems discarded, caps cut in half
150 g (5½ oz/1⅔ cups) shimeji mushrooms, separated

Serves 4 as part of a main

Combine the stock, oyster sauce and soy sauce in a small bowl and set aside.

Heat a wok over high heat and add the oil, swirling the oil around to coat the wok. Add the tofu and stir-fry for 3–4 minutes, or until the tofu starts to turn lightly golden. Pour off all but 1 tablespoon of oil from the wok, leaving the tofu in the wok.

Add the spring onions, ginger and garlic to the tofu. Stir-fry for 1 minute, then add all the mushrooms. Stir-fry for 1–2 minutes, or until the mushrooms just begin to wilt. Add the sauce mixture, pouring it down the side of the wok, and gently stir-fry for 1 minute to evenly coat all the mushrooms in the sauce. The mushrooms cook very quickly and will continue to cook after they are removed from the heat. Serve immediately.

The fermented bean curd used here is an exotic Chinatown ingredient and, some may say, an acquired taste. It adds a unique savoury, slightly salty flavour to this dish.

rice stick noodles with seafood

250 g (9 oz) dried rice stick noodles, 5 mm (¼ in) wide
2 tablespoons peanut oil
3 garlic cloves, finely chopped
1 teaspoon grated fresh ginger
3 spring onions (scallions), thinly sliced on the diagonal
1 tablespoon fermented tofu
12 raw large prawns (shrimp), peeled and deveined with tails intact
250 g (9 oz) firm white fish fillets, such as ling, blue eye or red fish, cut into 4 cm
    (1½ in) chunks
2 tablespoons shaoxing rice wine
200 g (7 oz) Chinese cabbage (wong bok), cut into 2 cm (¾ in) cubes
2–3 tablespoons light soy sauce
1 teaspoon sesame oil
1 spring onion (scallion), green part only, thinly sliced on the diagonal, to garnish

Serves 4 as a main

Put the noodles in a heatproof bowl, cover with boiling water and soak for 8–10 minutes. Rinse under cold water and drain well.

Heat a wok over high heat and add the oil, swirling the oil around to coat the wok. Add the garlic, ginger, spring onions and tofu and stir-fry for 30 seconds, ensuring the tofu is mashed up as you stir-fry. Add the prawns and fish and stir-fry for 2 minutes.

Add the rice wine, pouring it down the side of the wok, and allow it to sizzle for a few seconds. Add the cabbage, stir-fry for 1 minute, then add the soy sauce and noodles. Cook for 2 minutes, ensuring the sauce evenly coats the noodles. Serve with the sesame oil drizzled over the top and garnish with the spring onion.

This is a Chinatown twist on a classic dish, trout with almonds, which typically uses a whole trout. I have used trout fillet; the buttery almonds and the crisp celery complement the trout's rich yet delicate flesh.

trout with stir-fried almonds and celery

2 teaspoons light soy sauce
3 tablespoons chicken stock (page 187)
20 g (¾ oz) butter, cut into small cubes
500 ml (17 fl oz/2 cups) canola or vegetable oil, plus 1 extra tablespoon
400 g (14 oz) trout fillet, skin on
1 garlic clove, roughly chopped
2 spring onions (scallions), roughly chopped
25 g (1 oz/¼ cup) flaked almonds
2 celery stalks, thinly sliced on the diagonal
1 tablespoon flaked almonds, lightly toasted

Serves 2 as a main

Put the soy sauce, stock and butter in a small bowl and set aside.

Heat the oil in a wok over high heat. When the surface of the oil is shimmering, carefully lower the trout into the oil, skin side down. Cook for 4–5 minutes, carefully ladling some of the hot oil over the top, skinless side of the fillet. The fish is cooked when the skin is crisp and the flesh flakes easily. Remove and drain on paper towels.

Drain the oil from the wok, then wipe it clean with paper towels. Reheat the wok over high heat and add the extra oil, swirling the oil around to coat the wok. Add the garlic, spring onions and almonds and stir-fry for 1 minute. Add the celery and stir-fry for 1 minute, then add the sauce mixture, pouring it down the side of the wok. Cook for 2–3 minutes, or until the butter melts and the sauce has thickened.

Place the fish on a serving plate and spoon over the almond stir-fry and scatter over the toasted almonds.

These small, oval-shaped dried rice noodles are a truly unique Chinatown ingredient. There are a few varieties but be sure to use the dried ones that are slightly pliable.

duck with rice noodles and bamboo shoots

200 g (7 oz) dried oval rice noodles
185 ml (6 fl oz/¾ cup) chicken stock (page 187)
2 tablespoons oyster sauce
1 tablespoon light soy sauce
½ teaspoon caster (superfine) sugar
1 tablespoon peanut oil
1 garlic clove, chopped
1 teaspoon grated fresh ginger
½ Chinese barbecued duck, meat and skin cut into 1 cm (½ in) wide strips
125 g (4½ oz/½ cup) tinned, drained bamboo shoots, cut into 1 cm (½ in) wide strips
50 g (1¾ oz/½ bunch) garlic chives, cut into 3 cm (1¼ in) lengths

Serves 4 as part of a main

Bring a saucepan of water to the boil and cook the rice noodles for 5–6 minutes, or until they rise to the top of the water. Drain well and rinse under cold water.

Combine the stock, oyster sauce, soy sauce and sugar in a small bowl and stir for a few seconds to dissolve the sugar.

Heat a wok over high heat and add the oil, swirling the oil around to coat the wok. Add the garlic, ginger and duck and stir-fry for 1–2 minutes. Add the bamboo shoots and garlic chives and stir-fry for 1 minute. Add the sauce mixture, pouring it down the side of the wok, and cook for 2 minutes, gently stirring to combine all the ingredients. Add the noodles, gently stir-fry for 1 minute, then serve.

Hint: Oval rice noodles are small, flat noodles, about 2 cm (¾ in) long, and similar in shape to a coin or small disc. If unavailable, substitute fresh flat rice noodles.

Chinese food is not all about stir-frying, steaming and stovetop cooking. This recipe uses Western cooking techniques and Chinatown ingredients, making it a simple, put-in-the-oven-and-forget dish, with the classic flavour combination of beef and black bean.

beef and black bean casserole

1 kg (2 lb 4 oz) blade steak, cut into 4–5 cm (1½–2 in) pieces
60 g (2¼ oz/½ cup) plain (all-purpose) flour
1 teaspoon sesame oil
3 tablespoons peanut oil
1 large onion, cut into 5 mm (¼ in) thick slices
2 garlic cloves, peeled
4 slices fresh ginger
2 tablespoons salted black beans, rinsed
80 ml (2½ fl oz/⅓ cup) shaoxing rice wine
500 ml (17 fl oz/2 cups) chicken stock (page 187)
1 tablespoon light soy sauce
3 spring onions (scallions), thinly sliced on the diagonal into 3 cm (1¼ in) lengths
1 red chilli, thinly sliced on the diagonal

Serves 4 as a main

Preheat the oven to 180°C (350°F/Gas 4). Put the steak pieces in a large bowl with the flour and toss them around to evenly coat in the flour.

Heat the sesame oil and 1 tablespoon of the peanut oil in a heavy-based flameproof casserole dish or ovenproof saucepan. Add half of the meat to the dish and cook over medium heat for about 2 minutes each side, or until evenly browned. Put the cooked meat on a plate and repeat with the remaining meat. Remove the meat from the dish.

Add the remaining peanut oil and the onion to the dish and cook over medium heat for 5 minutes, or until the onion just begins to soften. Increase the heat to high and add the garlic, ginger and black beans. Cook for 1 minute, then pour in the rice wine and bring to a sizzle for 1 minute, or until most of the wine has evaporated. Return the meat to the dish. Add the stock and soy sauce and bring to the boil, stirring to combine all the ingredients and scraping up any cooked sediment on the bottom of the dish. Cover and put in the oven for 1½ hours, or until the meat is cooked and tender. Remove from the oven, take off the lid and place on the stovetop over high heat for 10 minutes to reduce and thicken the sauce a little. Scatter over the spring onions and chilli.

This dish pays homage to Chinese clay pot meals. If you have one, you could use the traditional clay pot to cook it in. Serve from the pot—remove the lid and release all the wonderful aromas at the table.

chinatown chicken casserole

100 g (3½ oz/½ cup) dried soya beans
900 g (2 lb) boneless, skinless chicken thighs, trimmed and cut in half
60 g (2¼ oz/½ cup) plain (all-purpose) flour
2 tablespoons peanut oil
2 teaspoons sesame oil
3 garlic cloves, peeled and lightly smashed with the flat side of a knife
4 thick slices fresh ginger
4 spring onions (scallions), cut into 3 cm (1¼ in) lengths
8 baby carrots
3 tablespoons shaoxing rice wine
500 ml (17 fl oz/2 cups) chicken stock (page 187)
3 tablespoons mushroom oyster sauce
½ teaspoon caster (superfine) sugar

Serves 4 as main

Soak the soya beans in cold water for 6–8 hours. Rub the beans with your fingers to remove the outer husks and rinse with cold water. Cook the beans in a large saucepan of boiling water for 1 hour. Drain and refrigerate until ready to use.

Toss the chicken in the flour. Heat half the peanut oil and half the sesame oil in a heavy-based flameproof casserole dish. Add half the chicken and cook over medium heat for 2–3 minutes each side, or until golden and just beginning to form a crust. Repeat with the remaining oils and chicken. Pour off the excess oil, leaving about 1 tablespoon in the dish.

Return all the chicken to the dish. Increase the heat to high and add the garlic, ginger, spring onions and carrots to the dish. Cook for 2 minutes, then add the rice wine. Sizzle for a couple of minutes, or until most of the wine has evaporated. Stir to combine all the cooking juices, scraping up any sediment on the bottom of the dish. Add the stock, oyster sauce, sugar and soya beans and bring to the boil. Reduce the heat and simmer, uncovered, for 30 minutes, stirring occasionally. Serve with rice or steamed Asian greens.

Hint: This casserole uses dried soya beans, which need to be soaked before use. If pressed for time, use 200 g (7 oz/1 cup) precooked tinned soya beans.

An omelette is truly comfort food at its best. Here it is given a Chinatown flavour by adding ingredients such as barbecued pork, ginger and soy sauce. For the sauce, it is important to use a good chicken stock. If not home-made, choose a shop-bought chicken stock that is light and not overly salty.

combination omelette

3 tablespoons peanut oil
200 g (7 oz) raw small prawns (shrimp), peeled and deveined
80 g (2¾ oz/1 small bunch) garlic chives, cut into 3 cm (1¼ in) lengths
2 handfuls bean sprouts
1 teaspoon grated fresh ginger
4 spring onions (scallions), thinly sliced on the diagonal
100 g (3½ oz) thinly sliced Chinese barbecued pork (char siu)
2 teaspoons cornflour (cornstarch)
2 teaspoons shaoxing rice wine
6 eggs, beaten
250 ml (9 fl oz/1 cup) chicken stock (page 187)
3 tablespoons oyster sauce

Serves 4 as a main

Heat 1 tablespoon of the oil in a frying pan or wok and cook the prawns over high heat for 1 minute each side. Add the garlic chives, bean sprouts, ginger and spring onions and stir-fry for 1 minute, or until the chives and sprouts begin to wilt. Put in a bowl and allow to cool. Add the pork, 1 teaspoon of the cornflour, the rice wine and a pinch of salt to the cooled mixture. Add the eggs and stir to combine.

Preheat the oven to 180°C (350°F/Gas 4). Heat 2 teaspoons of the oil in an 18 cm (7 in) non-stick frying pan over medium heat. Pour about 200 g (7 oz/1 cup) of the egg mixture into the pan, scattering the vegetables, prawns and pork evenly over the mixture. Cook for 2–3 minutes, or until the egg is set and browned underneath, then gently fold the omelette in half. Place on an ovenproof tray and put into the oven to keep warm while you cook three more omelettes.

Combine the remaining teaspoon of cornflour with the stock and oyster sauce in a small saucepan and bring to a gentle boil, stirring constantly until smooth and thickened slightly. Remove the omelettes from the oven and serve with the sauce.

Chinese barbecue shops are not limited to barbecued ducks and pork. They also have roasted meats, such as the soy-flavoured chicken used here. Under the dark soy-braised skin is the most succulent, full-flavoured chicken flesh.

soy chicken with rice noodles and garlic chives

1 Chinatown soy chicken
1 tablespoon Chinese chilli sauce
3 tablespoons chicken stock (page 187)
2 tablespoons oyster sauce
1 tablespoon light soy sauce
300 g (10½ oz) fresh rice noodles, 1 cm (½ in) wide
1 tablespoon peanut oil
1 garlic clove, roughly chopped
2 teaspoons grated fresh ginger
80 g (2¾ oz/1 small bunch) garlic chives, cut into 3 cm (1¼ in) lengths
2 handfuls bean sprouts

Serve 4 as a main

Remove the skin and meat from the chicken and cut both into 1 cm (½ in) strips. Combine the chilli sauce, stock, oyster sauce and soy sauce in a bowl.

Put the noodles in a colander and rinse under warm water for a few seconds, gently separating the noodles with your fingers. Drain well.

Heat the oil in a wok over high heat, swirling the oil around to coat the wok. Add the garlic and ginger and cook for 10 seconds, or until they just start to brown. Add the chicken and stir-fry for 2 minutes, then add the garlic chives and bean sprouts. Stir-fry for 2 minutes, or until the chives and sprouts begin to wilt. Add the noodles and gently toss the ingredients together for a minute. Add the sauce mixture, pouring it down the side of the wok, and cook for 2–3 minutes, gently tossing until the noodles are coated in the sauce.

The salted black soya bean is one of the oldest soy foods and was used as a seasoning long before soy sauce. They are also sold with the addition of ginger, orange peel or five-spice but I prefer the unflavoured variety.

fish with black beans and ginger

1 tablespoon peanut oil
30 g (1 oz) fresh ginger, julienned
4 spring onions (scallions), very thinly sliced on the diagonal
1 red chilli, cut in half lengthways
2 tablespoons salted black beans, rinsed and roughly mashed
2 tablespoons shaoxing rice wine
2 teaspoons caster (superfine) sugar
1 tablespoon Chinese black vinegar
3 tablespoons chicken stock (page 187)
2 x 400 g (14 oz) whole snapper (or firm, white-fleshed fish), gutted and scaled
2 tablespoons cornflour (cornstarch)
canola or vegetable oil, for deep-frying

Serves 2 as a main

Heat the peanut oil in a small saucepan over high heat. When the oil just reaches smoking point, add the ginger, spring onions, chilli and black beans and cook for 30 seconds. Add the rice wine, sugar, vinegar and stock and bring to the boil. Simmer for 2 minutes, then remove to a bowl.

Score the fish three to four times on each side. Put the cornflour on a plate and toss the fish in the cornflour to evenly coat.

Fill a wok two-thirds full with the oil and heat over medium–high heat. When the surface of the oil is shimmering, hold the fish by its tail and gently and carefully lower it into the oil and cook for 3–4 minutes. Carefully turn the fish over and cook for a further 2–3 minutes, basting with the hot oil. The fish is cooked when the flesh flakes easily with a fork and the skin is lightly golden. Remove and drain on paper towels for a couple of minutes. Repeat for the second fish. Place the fish on serving plates and pour over the black bean sauce.

The simple marinade used here creates a dark, roasted skin over succulent flesh—a perfect roast chicken with authentic Chinatown flavours.

soy roast chicken with ginger and spring onion

1.6 kg (3 lb 8 oz) chicken
1 tablespoon dark soy sauce
2 teaspoons sesame oil
3 tablespoons light soy sauce
2 tablespoons shaoxing rice wine
1 teaspoon caster (superfine) sugar
3 tablespoons chicken stock (page 187)
2 tablespoons finely shredded fresh ginger
4 spring onions (scallions), thinly sliced on the diagonal
2 tablespoons peanut oil

Serves 4 as a main

Wash the chicken and dry with paper towels. Combine the dark soy sauce and 1 teaspoon of the sesame oil in a small bowl and rub the mixture all over the chicken. Place the chicken in a large bowl, uncovered, and refrigerate for a few hours, or preferably overnight, turning the chicken occasionally.

Preheat the oven to 200°C (400°F/Gas 6) and line a roasting tin with baking paper. Put the chicken, breast side up, in the tin and cook for 20 minutes. Turn the chicken over and cook for another 20 minutes. Finally, turn the chicken over, so that it is breast side up again, and cook for 30 minutes, or until the chicken is golden brown and tender and the juices run clear when the thigh is pierced with a skewer. Remove and allow to cool slightly, then cut into 10 small pieces. To do this, use kitchen scissors to cut the chicken in half down the length of the breastbone. Gently remove the legs and wings, then cut each breast piece into 3 equal pieces. Place on a serving platter.

Put the light soy sauce, rice wine, sugar and stock in a small saucepan and gently heat for 2–3 minutes. Pour the sauce mixture over the chicken pieces, then scatter with the ginger and spring onions.

Wipe the saucepan dry with paper towels, then put the peanut oil and remaining sesame oil in the pan over high heat. When the oil reaches smoking point, carefully pour it over the chicken, which will cause the ginger and spring onion to sizzle. Serve immediately.

In Chinatown you will find many brands of dried, fermented black beans. They vary greatly in their saltiness, so it is a good idea to rinse them before use.

black bean and chilli chicken with leeks

900 g (2 lb) boneless, skinless chicken thighs, trimmed and cut in half
3 tablespoons shaoxing rice wine
125 ml (4 fl oz/½ cup) chicken stock (page 187)
1 teaspoon caster (superfine) sugar
1 tablespoon Chinese black vinegar
2 tablespoons oyster sauce
3 tablespoons peanut oil
2 tablespoons julienned fresh ginger
2 garlic cloves, roughly chopped
1 large leek, white part only, julienned
2 tablespoons salted black beans, rinsed and roughly mashed
3 red chillies, thinly sliced on the diagonal
coriander (cilantro) sprigs, to garnish

Serves 4 as a main

Put the chicken in a non-metallic bowl with 1 tablespoon of the rice wine and refrigerate for a few hours. Combine the stock, sugar, vinegar and oyster sauce in a small bowl.

Heat 2 tablespoons of the oil in a wok over high heat, swirling the oil around to coat the wok. When the oil reaches smoking point, add half the chicken, making sure the pieces do not overlap, and cook for 1 minute, without moving the chicken. Turn the chicken over and cook for 1 minute, again without moving it. This will give the chicken a nice golden crust. After this time, shake the wok around for 1 minute, moving the chicken pieces up and around the top of the wok. The chicken should be browned and partially cooked. Remove to a plate. Cook the rest of the chicken the same way, adding more oil if needed.

Add the remaining oil to the wok and, leaving the wok on high heat, add the ginger, garlic, leek, black beans and chillies and stir-fry for 1 minute. Add the remaining rice wine, pouring it down the side of the wok, and allow to sizzle for a few seconds. Return the chicken to the wok, then add the sauce mixture and stir-fry for 3–4 minutes, or until the sauce thickens and coats the ingredients. Garnish with the coriander sprigs.

spice

This is a spicy chicken version of san choy bau, which roughly translates as 'raw vegetable'. The crispy, fresh lettuce is wrapped around a tasty stir-fry and topped with pine nuts, a variety of which is native to China.

spicy chicken in lettuce cups

500 g (1 lb 2 oz) boneless, skinless chicken thighs, trimmed and roughly chopped
2 tablespoons shaoxing rice wine
4 small dried shiitake mushrooms
½ teaspoon caster (superfine) sugar
80 ml (2½ fl oz/⅓ cup) chicken stock (page 187)
1 tablespoon oyster sauce
1 tablespoon peanut oil
1 garlic clove, roughly chopped
1 teaspoon grated fresh ginger
2 spring onions (scallions), white part chopped and green part thinly sliced
2 small red chillies, finely chopped
2 tablespoons pine nuts
40 g (1½ oz/¼ cup) water chestnuts, roughly chopped
8 iceberg lettuce leaves, washed

Serves 4 as a starter

Put the chicken and 1 tablespoon of the rice wine into a food processor and process until the chicken is finely chopped. Refrigerate for a few hours, or until ready to use.

Put the dried mushrooms in a bowl, cover with boiling water and soak for 20–30 minutes. Squeeze out the excess liquid from the mushrooms, then remove and discard the stems and finely chop the caps. Reserve 60 ml (2 fl oz/¼ cup) of the soaking liquid. Combine the sugar, stock, oyster sauce, remaining rice wine and the reserved mushroom soaking liquid in a bowl, stirring to dissolve the sugar.

Heat a wok over high heat and add the oil, swirling the oil around to coat the wok. When the oil reaches smoking point, add the garlic, ginger, spring onion whites and chillies and cook for a few seconds. Add the chicken and half the pine nuts and stir-fry for 3–4 minutes, or until the chicken is almost cooked, stirring constantly to break up the chicken. Add the mushrooms and water chestnuts and stir-fry for 1 minute. Add the sauce mixture, pouring it down the side of the wok, and bring to the boil for 2–3 minutes, or until the sauce has almost evaporated. Serve in a bowl, sprinkled with the spring onion greens, the remaining pine nuts, and with the lettuce on the side. Assemble these at the table, two per person.

While salt brings out the natural sweetness of the prawn, the chilli adds complexity and bite.

salt and chilli prawns

12 raw large prawns (shrimp)
3 tablespoons vegetable oil
4 garlic cloves, crushed
2 teaspoons sea salt flakes
2 teaspoons chilli flakes
1 lemon, cut into wedges

Serves 4 as a starter

To remove the vein without peeling the prawn, make an incision on the back of the prawn, just behind the head, and another incision just above the tail. Use a toothpick or a pair of kitchen tweezers to slowly pull up and remove the vein from the incision behind the head. On large prawns the vein should come out easily. Put the prawns in a bowl with the oil and garlic and toss the prawns to evenly coat them in the marinade. Refrigerate for 1 hour.

Preheat a chargrill pan or barbecue to high. Remove the prawns from the marinade and shake off any excess. Cook the prawns, brushing them with a little of the marinade, for 2–3 minutes each side, or until they turn pink and are cooked through.

Put the sea salt and chilli flakes in a large bowl. Add the cooked prawns and toss around for a few seconds to evenly coat the prawns in the salt and chilli mixture. Serve with a wedge of lemon to squeeze over the prawns.

This is a beautiful soup—it has a wonderfully delicate, light flavour, subtly spiced with white pepper. White pepper has more of a peppery 'bite' than black pepper, so should be used sparingly.

tomato eggflower soup

1 litre (35 fl oz/4 cups) chicken stock (page 187)
6 thin slices fresh ginger
3 firm tomatoes, cut into small wedges
1 tablespoon light soy sauce
1 teaspoon caster (superfine) sugar
½ teaspoon ground white pepper
sea salt flakes
1 egg white, lightly beaten
1 spring onion (scallion), thinly sliced on the diagonal
coriander (cilantro) sprigs, to garnish
1 teaspoon sesame oil

Serves 4 as a starter

Put the stock and ginger in a large saucepan and bring to the boil for 2–3 minutes. Add the tomatoes, soy sauce, sugar, white pepper and a generous pinch of sea salt. Bring to the boil, then turn off the heat.

Slowly pour the egg white into the soup, pouring it in a steady stream, stirring the soup as you do this. Rest for 1 minute, then serve in small bowls. Garnish with the spring onion and coriander sprigs and drizzle with a little sesame oil.

This recipe combines Chinatown ingredients and flavours with a Middle-Eastern inspired serving suggestion.

cumin lamb skewers

400 g (14 oz) lamb loin fillets, cut into bite-sized cubes
1 teaspoon sesame oil
1 garlic clove, finely chopped
2 teaspoons chilli flakes
1 teaspoon ground cumin
2 tablespoons Chinese barbecue (char siu) sauce
8 peking duck (mandarin) pancakes
1 small Lebanese (short) cucumber, julienned
2–3 spring onions (scallions), thinly sliced on the diagonal into 5 cm (2 in) lengths
½ teaspoon sea salt flakes
1 lemon, cut into wedges

Serves 4 as a starter

Put the lamb in a bowl with the sesame oil, garlic, chilli flakes and ½ teaspoon of the cumin and toss to coat the lamb in the marinade. Refrigerate for a few hours, or overnight.

Soak 8 bamboo skewers in water for 1 hour to prevent them burning. Preheat the oven to 180°C (350°F/Gas 4). Put the barbecue sauce in a small bowl with 2 teaspoons warm water, stir until smooth and set aside.

Wrap the pancakes in cooking foil and warm in the oven while you cook the lamb. Preheat a chargrill pan or barbecue chargrill plate to high. Put four pieces of lamb onto each bamboo skewer and cook the lamb for 6–8 minutes, turning every couple of minutes, or until the lamb is well browned and cooked to your liking.

To serve, spread a little of the sauce on a pancake, top with the lamb from a skewer and some cucumber and spring onions. Mix the sea salt and remaining cumin and sprinkle over the top. Squeeze over some lemon juice and roll up the pancake.

The great thing about fried rice is you can put just about anything in it you fancy. It can be a meal on its own or a lighter affair, like this version, to accompany other dishes, especially barbecued meats.

cashew and chilli fried rice

2 tablespoons peanut oil
100 g (3½ oz/⅔ cup) cashews, dry-roasted
2 teaspoons grated fresh ginger
1 garlic clove, roughly chopped
2 spring onions (scallions), roughly chopped
2–3 small red chillies, finely chopped
550 g (1 lb 4 oz/3 cups) cooked, cooled long-grain rice
1 tablespoon light soy sauce

Serves 4 as part of a main

Heat a wok over high heat and add 1 tablespoon of the oil, swirling the oil around to coat the wok. Add the cashews, ginger, garlic, spring onions and chillies to the wok and stir-fry for 2 minutes. Add the cooked rice and stir-fry for 5 minutes. Add the soy sauce, pouring it down the side of the wok, and stir-fry for 1 minute to combine.

Hint: For 550 g (1 lb 4 oz/3 cups) cooked long-grain rice, you will need 200 g (7 oz/1 cup) raw rice. Allow the rice to cool thoroughly before using it.

Potatoes are a very popular ingredient in Western cooking. In this recipe we get the best of both worlds: lightly golden, crispy potatoes seasoned with the spices of Chinatown. These spicy potatoes are also excellent served with a cold beer as a starter.

salt and pepper potatoes

1 kg (2 lb 4 oz) roasting potatoes, such as desiree, peeled and cut into 2 cm (¾ in) pieces
500 ml (17 fl oz/2 cups) peanut oil
1 large green chilli, seeded and finely chopped
1 large red chilli, seeded and finely chopped
1 garlic clove, finely chopped
1 small handful coriander (cilantro) leaves, roughly chopped
1 teaspoon sichuan pepper and salt mixture (page 187)
1 lemon, cut into wedges

Serves 4 as part of a main

Put the potatoes in a large saucepan of cold water. Bring to the boil and cook for 1 minute. Remove from the heat and drain the potatoes. Put the potatoes in a single layer on a flat tray for a few hours to dry out.

Heat the oil in a wok over high heat. When the surface of the oil is shimmering, add the potatoes, cooking them in batches, and deep-fry for 4–5 minutes, or until they just begin to turn golden. Remove the potatoes from the wok and drain on paper towels. Drain off all but 1 tablespoon of oil. Add the chillies and garlic and stir-fry for a few seconds. Return the potatoes to the wok and stir-fry for 1 minute to evenly coat the potatoes in the chilli mixture. Remove from the heat, stir in the coriander and serve sprinkled with the pepper and salt mixture, and wedges of lemon to squeeze over.

Small bags of sichuan peppercorns were once used as a gift to express affection. Here they are combined with salt to make a great seasoning for barbecued foods.

salt and chilli sweet corn

1 tablespoon peanut oil
4 corn cobs
50 g (1¾ oz) butter
1 teaspoon sichuan pepper and salt mixture (page 187)
1 teaspoon chilli flakes

Serves 4 as part of a main

Heat the oil in a frying pan over medium heat. Cook the corn for 10–12 minutes, turning every couple of minutes. The corn should be evenly golden. Add half of the butter to the pan and cook for 2–3 minutes, turning the corn around in the melted butter.

Arrange the corn on a plate and sprinkle over the pepper and salt mixture and chilli flakes, then top with the remaining butter.

Shanghai noodles have a wonderful fresh, floury smell. They are made commercially and are generally sold fresh and uncooked. Watching them being made the traditional way, by hand, is quite a spectacle, which can often be seen in northern-style Chinese restaurants.

duck and star anise broth with Shanghai noodles

½ Chinese barbecued duck
2 star anise
½ teaspoon sichuan peppercorns
8 small dried shiitake mushrooms
3 tablespoons soy sauce
750 g (1 lb 10 oz/1 bunch) Chinese broccoli (gai larn), chopped into
    3–4 cm (1¼–1½ in) lengths
6 thin slices fresh ginger
300 g (10½ oz) fresh shanghai noodles

Serves 4 as a main

Remove the skin and meat from the duck and cut both into 2 cm (¾ in) pieces. Set aside.

Put the duck carcass in a large saucepan with the star anise, peppercorns, mushrooms, soy sauce and 2 litres (70 fl oz/8 cups) water. Bring to the boil, then reduce the heat and gently simmer for 45 minutes.

Strain the stock into another large saucepan. Remove and discard the stems from the mushrooms and add the mushroom caps to the strained broth. Discard the other stock ingredients (reserving the star anise and peppercorns for garnish, if you like). Add the Chinese broccoli and ginger to the stock, then place over low heat to keep warm.

Bring a saucepan of water to the boil and add the noodles. Cook for 8–10 minutes, or until the noodles rise to the top of the water and are tender. Drain and divide between four serving bowls. Ladle over the hot broth and evenly divide the other ingredients between the four bowls. Place the duck pieces on top.

Although it isn't native to China, the fennel seed is often used in Chinese cooking—its aniseed flavour is lovely with roasted pork. This recipe makes use of the technique of rubbing the skin with vinegar and salt prior to cooking, producing a perfect 'crackling' skin.

roasted pork loin with fennel and soy

1 kg (2 lb 4 oz) piece of pork loin, skin on
2 tablespoons Chinese rice vinegar
1 tablespoon sea salt flakes
2 teaspoons fennel seeds, roughly crushed
1 garlic clove, finely chopped
2 tablespoons light soy sauce

Serves 4 as a main

Using a sharp knife, make incisions in the skin of the pork about 1 cm (½ in) apart, cutting almost through to the meat. Rub the vinegar and sea salt over the skin side of the pork and set aside for 1 hour, leaving the pork at room temperature.

Preheat the oven to 220°C (425°F/Gas 7). Rub the fennel and garlic into the skin of the pork, being sure to rub it into the incisions in the skin. Place in a roasting tin and pour the soy sauce and 250 ml (9 fl oz/1 cup) water into the bottom of the tin, but not over the pork itself. Cook for 30 minutes. After this time, reduce the oven to 160°C (315°F/Gas 2–3) and roast for a further 2 hours, or until the pork skin is dark golden and crisp on top and the meat is cooked through.

Remove the pork from the oven, transfer to a clean tray and place, skin side up, under a hot griller (broiler) for 2–4 minutes, or until the skin is puffed and crispy. (Position the pork so that it is about 5 cm (2 in) away from the griller or the skin will burn too quickly.) Remove the pork and set aside to rest for 5 minutes. Cut into 1 cm (½ in) wide strips and serve with steamed Asian greens.

Before cooking tofu it is a good idea to use paper towels to absorb some of the tofu's excess moisture. This way, the tofu stays firm and is less likely to break up when cooked.

salt and pepper tofu

600 g (1 lb 5 oz) block silken tofu
750 ml (26 fl oz/3 cups) canola or vegetable oil
60 g (2^1/$_4$ oz/^{1}/$_2$ cup) cornflour (cornstarch)
1–2 teaspoons sichuan pepper and salt mixture (page 187)
1 lemon, cut into wedges

Serves 4 as part of a main

Cut the tofu into 16 cubes and carefully put the cubes onto a plate lined with a couple of layers of paper towel. Place a couple more layers of paper towel on top and leave for about 30 minutes to allow the excess liquid to be absorbed. Put the drained tofu on a dry sheet of paper towel.

Heat the oil in a wok over high heat. The oil is hot enough when the surface starts to shimmer. Put the cornflour in a bowl. Rolling each piece of tofu in the cornflour just before you fry it, carefully lower the tofu into the hot oil using tongs. Cook the tofu in batches for 1 minute, or until it is light golden in colour. Remove and place on paper towels to drain.

Sprinkle with the pepper and salt mixture, to taste. Serve immediately, with a lemon wedge for squeezing over the tofu.

The malty, richly flavoured black vinegars from Chinkiang are considered superior for use, and feature predominantly in northern Chinese cooking. Here the vinegar is partnered with cumin, giving the lamb a slight Middle Eastern feel.

roast lamb with cumin and black vinegar

1½–2 teaspoons cumin seeds
½ teaspoon black peppercorns
½ teaspoon sea salt flakes
600 g (1 lb 5 oz) lamb backstraps or lamb loin fillets
125 ml (4 fl oz/½ cup) chicken stock (page 187)
1 tablespoon light soy sauce
1 tablespoon Chinese black vinegar
½ teaspoon caster (superfine) sugar
8 baby leeks, ends trimmed, cut in half
1 teaspoon peanut oil

Serves 4 as a main

Using a mortar and pestle, crush the cumin seeds, peppercorns and sea salt to a rough powder. Rub the spice mixture all over the lamb and set aside for about 1 hour, leaving the lamb at room temperature.

Combine the stock, soy sauce, vinegar and sugar in a small bowl and set aside. Preheat the oven to 220°C (425°F/Gas 7). Arrange the leeks in the centre of a roasting tin.

Heat the oil in a frying pan over high heat and brown the lamb for 1 minute each side. Put the lamb on top of the leeks. Pour the sauce mixture into the tin and roast in the oven for 10–15 minutes, or until the lamb is cooked to your liking. Remove from the oven and put the lamb and leeks on a chopping board and leave to rest for 5 minutes.

Pour the cooking juices into a small saucepan and bring to the boil for 3–4 minutes. Slice the lamb and serve with the roasted leeks. Pour over the sauce.

Have you ever wondered why your stir-fried chicken is not as tender as the restaurant version? Chances are that the chef would have used the technique referred to as 'velveting' to tenderize the meat. To do this, the chicken is marinated in a rice wine mixture and then blanched in hot water or oil before cooking. It is well worth the extra effort.

velveted chicken with cashews and smoky chilli

1 tablespoon shaoxing rice wine
1 tablespoon cornflour (cornstarch)
1 egg white
500 g (1 lb 2 oz) boneless, skinless chicken breast, cut into 1 cm (½ in) wide strips
125 ml (4 fl oz/½ cup) chicken stock (page 187)
1 tablespoon light soy sauce
1 tablespoon oyster sauce
2 tablespoons peanut oil
4 large dried red chillies
1 garlic clove, finely chopped
1 teaspoon grated fresh ginger
2 spring onions (scallions), finely chopped
80 g (2¾ oz/½ cup) cashews, dry-roasted

Serves 4 as a main

Put the rice wine, cornflour and egg white with a pinch of salt in a small food processor and process for 1 minute to form a thick white mixture. Alternatively, whisk the ingredients together in a bowl. Put the chicken in a non-metallic bowl and toss it in the mixture to evenly coat. Cover and refrigerate for a few hours, or overnight.

Combine the stock, soy sauce and oyster sauce in a bowl and set aside.

Bring a large saucepan of water to boil, add half the chicken pieces and cook for 1 minute, stirring. Remove, shaking off the excess liquid. Repeat with the remaining chicken.

Heat a wok over high heat and add the oil, swirling the oil around to coat the wok. Add the chillies and cook for a few seconds, or until they begin to darken and give off a smoky aroma. Add the garlic, ginger, spring onions and cashews and stir-fry for a few seconds. Add the chicken and stir-fry for 1–2 minutes. Pour in the sauce mixture and bring to the boil for 2–3 minutes, or until the sauce has almost evaporated and coats the chicken.

This dish uses both white and black pepper—the flavour is slightly reminiscent of the Western-style peppered steak.

peppered beef and shiitake with rice noodles

½ teaspoon black peppercorns
½ teaspoon white peppercorns
3 tablespoons chicken stock (page 187)
2 tablespoons shaoxing rice wine
3 tablespoons mushroom oyster sauce
2 tablespoons light soy sauce
1 tablespoon caster (superfine) sugar
500 g (1 lb 2 oz) fresh rice noodles, cut into 3 cm (1¼ in) wide strips
3 tablespoons peanut oil
1 garlic clove, roughly chopped
1 teaspoon grated fresh ginger
200 g (7 oz) beef fillet, thinly sliced across the grain
6 shiitake mushrooms, stems discarded and caps cut in half
100 g (3½ oz) Chinese broccoli (gai larn), chopped into 5 cm (2 in) lengths

Serves 4 as a main

Put the black and white peppercorns in a dry frying pan over high heat for 1–2 minutes, or until they begin to smoke or crackle. When cool, use a mortar and pestle to grind the peppercorns to a rough powder.

Combine the stock, rice wine, mushroom oyster sauce, soy sauce and sugar in a bowl and stir to dissolve the sugar. Put the noodles in a colander and rinse under warm water for a few seconds, gently separating the noodles with your fingers. Drain well.

Heat a wok over high heat and add the oil. When the oil has just reached smoking point, add the garlic, ginger and half of the peppercorn mixture. Stir-fry for a few seconds. Add the beef and stir-fry for 1 minute, then pour in the sauce mixture and bring to the boil for 1 minute. Add the mushrooms and Chinese broccoli and stir-fry for 1 minute, then add the noodles and gently toss the ingredients around in the wok for 2 minutes. Arrange on a serving plate and sprinkle with the remaining ground pepper.

Chilli oil is common in Sichuan cooking where it is simply called 'red oil' after its magnificent colour. But like all flavoured oils it can go stale and lose its potency, so store in a cool, dry place away from direct sunlight.

seared kingfish with orange and chilli oil

2 tablespoons shaoxing rice wine
2 tablespoons light soy sauce
½ teaspoon caster (superfine) sugar
2 tablespoons peanut oil
1 large, thick kingfish or swordfish cutlet, about 500 g (1 lb 2 oz)
2 tablespoons finely shredded fresh ginger
2 spring onions (scallions), thinly sliced on the diagonal into long lengths
1 teaspoon finely grated orange zest
2 teaspoons Chinese chilli oil

Serves 4 as a main

Combine the rice wine, soy sauce, sugar and 1 tablespoon water in a small bowl and stir for a few seconds to dissolve the sugar.

Heat a heavy-based frying pan over high heat and add 1 tablespoon of the oil, swirling the oil around to coat the bottom of the pan. Add the fish and cook for 1–2 minutes, or until a dark golden crust has formed. Turn over and cook for 4 minutes. Add the sauce mixture to the pan to heat through. Remove the fish to a plate and pour the sauce around the fish. Sprinkle the ginger, spring onions and orange zest over the top of the fish.

Heat the chilli oil and remaining peanut oil in a small saucepan until the oil reaches smoking point, then pour the hot oil over the top of the fish, causing the ginger, spring onion and orange zest to sizzle.

This wonderful salad is a version of a northern Chinese speciality. The flavour is slightly salty and has a mild numbing effect on the mouth due to the sichuan peppercorns. And it has quite a chilli kick.

spiced chicken salad

1 teaspoon sichuan peppercorns
1 Chinatown soy chicken
6 spring onions (scallions), thinly sliced on the diagonal into long lengths
1 Lebanese (short) cucumber, seeds removed, thinly sliced on the diagonal
2 teaspoons caster (superfine) sugar
2 tablespoons light soy sauce
3 teaspoons Chinese chilli oil
2 teaspoons sesame oil

Serves 4 as a main

Put the peppercorns in a dry frying pan over medium heat for 2–3 minutes, or until they begin to smoke or crackle. Remove and place in a bowl. When cool, use a mortar and pestle to grind the peppercorns to a rough powder.

Remove the skin from the chicken and discard. Using a fork, finely shred the chicken meat and put in a bowl with the spring onions and cucumber.

Combine the sugar and soy sauce in a bowl and stir to dissolve the sugar. Whisk in the chilli oil and sesame oil, then pour over the chicken. Toss around to evenly coat the chicken in the dressing. Serve on a platter or in individual bowls and sprinkle over the ground pepper.

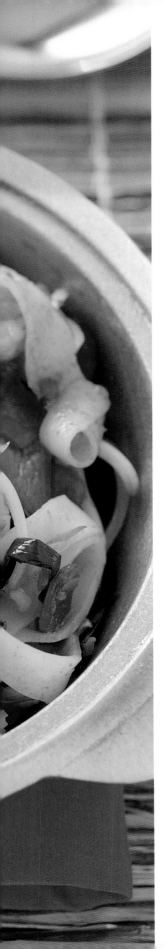

One of my all time favourites, this wonderful spicy noodle dish has a Singaporean influence but uses Chinatown ingredients, including lap cheong sausage and fiery Chinese chilli sauce.

char kway teow

2 lap cheong sausages
400 g (14 oz) fresh rice noodles, cut into 1 cm (½ in) wide strips
1 tablespoon Chinese chilli sauce
2 tablespoons light soy sauce
3 tablespoons chicken stock (page 187)
1 tablespoon peanut oil
1 garlic clove, roughly chopped
2 teaspoons grated fresh ginger
3 spring onions (scallions), chopped
1–2 large red chillies, seeded and chopped
12 raw small to medium prawns (shrimp), peeled and deveined with tails intact
100 g (3½ oz) Chinese barbecued pork (char siu), cut into thin slices
2 handfuls bean sprouts
50 g (1¾ oz/½ bunch) garlic chives, cut into 3 cm (1¼ in) lengths

Serves 4 as a main

Put the sausages in a heatproof bowl and pour over boiling water to cover. Leave for 10 minutes. Remove the sausages and slice thinly.

Put the noodles in a colander and rinse under warm water for a few seconds, gently separating the noodles with your fingers. Drain well. Combine the chilli sauce, soy sauce and stock in a small bowl.

Heat the oil in a wok over high heat, swirling the oil around to coat the wok. When the oil reaches smoking point, add the garlic, ginger, spring onions, chillies and sausage slices and stir-fry for 30 seconds. Add the prawns and stir-fry for 1 minute. Add the pork, bean sprouts and garlic chives and stir-fry for 2 minutes, then add the noodles and gently toss the ingredients to combine. Add the sauce mixture, pouring it down the side of the wok, and bring to a sizzling boil for 2–3 minutes, without stirring. At this point the sauce should begin to evaporate. Stir for 1 minute, then serve.

This is very much a hands-on affair, so provide finger bowls and napkins. A tip for really spicy food—eat it with steamed rice, as this helps diffuse the heat.

chilli blue swimmer crab

4 blue swimmer crabs
3 tablespoons Chinese chilli sauce
3 tablespoons tomato sauce (ketchup)
185 ml (6 fl oz/³⁄₄ cup) chicken stock (page 187)
1 teaspoon caster (superfine) sugar
125 ml (4 fl oz/¹⁄₂ cup) canola or vegetable oil
2 garlic cloves, roughly chopped
1 tablespoon grated fresh ginger
2 spring onions (scallions), white part chopped and green part sliced on the diagonal
2 large red chillies, thinly sliced on the diagonal
1 egg, lightly beaten

Serves 4 as a main

If live, put the crabs in the freezer for 1 hour before preparing them. Using a cleaver or heavy-bladed knife, make an incision through the head of the crab. Put the crabs on their backs and lift up the tail apron. Using your thumb, lever off the top shell. Remove the spongy grey gill tissue and intestines. Rinse the crab under cold water and dry well with paper towels. Using the cleaver, cut the crab in half. Cut each of these halves, between the legs, to give four portions per crab. Crack the claws using the flat edge of the cleaver or with a meat mallet (to help the flavour penetrate the crab meat). Refrigerate until ready to cook.

Combine the chilli sauce, tomato sauce, stock and sugar in a bowl and stir to dissolve the sugar. Set aside.

Heat the oil in a wok over high heat. When the oil reaches smoking point, add half of the crab to the wok and cook for 3–4 minutes, using kitchen tongs to carefully toss the crab in the oil, until the crab is evenly coloured. Repeat with the remaining crab, then set aside.

Drain all but 1 tablespoon of oil from the wok. Add the garlic, ginger, spring onion whites and half the chillies and cook for 10 seconds over high heat, being careful not to burn them. Return the crab to the wok, along with the sauce mixture, bring to the boil and cook for 3 minutes, tossing the crab to coat in the sauce. Slowly pour the egg into the wok in a steady stream, stirring as you do this. Cook for 1 minute. Serve scattered with the remaining chilli and spring onion greens. Crab is best eaten with your hands, so provide finger bowls.

Chilli oil is the spicy fusion of chillies and oil. It has an unmistakable colour (bright red) and flavour (fiery hot). If you do like it hot, add a few more drops (or teaspoons) to the sauce.

steamed salmon with chilli oil

2 tablespoons shaoxing rice wine
2 tablespoons light soy sauce
½ teaspoon caster (superfine) sugar
1 teaspoon Chinese chilli oil
400 g (14 oz) salmon fillet, mid cut
2 spring onions (scallions), thinly sliced on the diagonal
2 tablespoons thinly sliced fresh ginger
1 tablespoon peanut oil
1 teaspoon sesame oil
2–3 coriander (cilantro) sprigs

Serves 4 as a part of a main

Combine the rice wine, soy sauce, sugar and chilli oil in a bowl and stir to dissolve the sugar.

Bring a wok or large saucepan of water to the boil. Put the salmon in a heatproof bowl and put into a large bamboo steamer. Pour the sauce mixture over the salmon, put a lid on the steamer and steam over boiling water for 6–8 minutes, or until the salmon is cooked and the flesh flakes easily with a fork. Carefully remove the salmon and sprinkle over the spring onions and ginger.

Heat the peanut oil and sesame oil in a small saucepan over high heat. When the oil reaches smoking point, pour the oil evenly over the fish, sizzling the spring onions and ginger. Garnish with the coriander sprigs and serve.

I love the way rice is cooked in India, pilau in particular. The end result defies its simplicity. This is a dead-easy, Chinatown version of pilau, with the ubiquitous Chinese chilli–garlic sauce giving it its kick. Although not traditionally Chinese, the lime juice is a zesty addition.

chinatown pilau

1 tablespoon peanut oil
1 small red onion, finely chopped
2 tablespoons Chinese chilli–garlic sauce
1 teaspoon freshly grated turmeric
200 g (7 oz/1 cup) long-grain rice
375 ml (13 fl oz/1½ cups) chicken stock (page 187)
2 tablespoons light soy sauce
1 tablespoon lime juice
2 tablespoons roughly chopped coriander (cilantro) leaves

Serves 4 as part of a main

Heat the oil in a saucepan over medium heat. Add the onion and cook for 3–5 minutes, or until the onion has softened. Stir in the chilli–garlic sauce and turmeric and cook for a further 2–3 minutes, or until evenly combined and aromatic.

Add the rice, stir to combine well, then pour in the stock. Bring to the boil, stir once, then reduce the heat to low. Cover the pan with a tight-fitting lid and cook over very low heat for 20–25 minutes, or until the rice is tender and cooked through. Remove from the heat and stir in the soy sauce, lime juice and coriander.

Hint: You should be able to find fresh turmeric in your local Chinatown. If unavailable, substitute ¼ teaspoon ground turmeric.

Salt and pepper is the universal seasoning combination. You will see white and black pepper in Chinese cooking, but they have never replaced the use of the piquant sichuan peppercorn, which is more mouth-numbing than it is peppery-hot.

salt and pepper trout with cucumber salad

2 x 500 g (1 lb 2 oz) rainbow trout
750 ml (26 fl oz/3 cups) canola or vegetable oil
1 large red chilli, very thinly sliced on the diagonal
1 large green chilli, very thinly sliced on the diagonal
1 Lebanese (short) cucumber, seeds removed and thinly sliced
½ iceberg lettuce, cut into 2–3 cm (¾–1¼ in) pieces
2 spring onions (scallions), sliced on the diagonal
2 tablespoons peanut oil
1 tablespoon Chinese rice vinegar
½ teaspoon caster (superfine) sugar
1½ teaspoons sichuan pepper and salt mixture (page 187)
1 lemon, cut into wedges

Serves 4 as a main

Wash the fish and pat dry with paper towels. Score the fish three to four times on each side.

Heat the oil in a large wok over high heat. When the surface of the oil is shimmering, add the red and green chillies and cook for a few seconds. Remove and drain on paper towels.

Carefully add both fish to the wok and fry for 3–4 minutes, ladling the hot oil over the fish. Turn over and cook for 2 minutes on the other side, or until the skin is crispy and dark golden and the flesh flakes easily with a fork. Drain on paper towels, then place on a serving plate.

Put the cucumber and lettuce in a bowl and top with the spring onions and fried chillies. To make a dressing, combine the peanut oil, vinegar and sugar in a small bowl, stirring to dissolve the sugar. Pour the dressing over the salad. Sprinkle the pepper and salt mixture over the fish and the salad and serve with a wedge of lemon.

The hot, smoky flavours of this stir-fry provided the inspiration for the title. But, beware, heat can vary with dried chillies.

gunpowder chicken

850 g (1 lb 14 oz) boneless, skinless chicken thighs, trimmed, each thigh cut
    into 4 pieces
1 tablespoon shaoxing rice wine
3 tablespoons soy sauce
1 tablespoon cornflour (cornstarch)
2 tablespoons Chinese black vinegar
2 tablespoons chicken stock (page 187)
2 teaspoons caster (superfine) sugar
8 small dried red chillies
2 tablespoons canola or vegetable oil
1/2 teaspoon ground sichuan peppercorns
1 small red capsicum (pepper), cut into 2 cm (3/4 in) cubes
3 tablespoons peanuts, skin on

Serves 4 as a main

Put the chicken in a non-metallic bowl with the rice wine and 1 tablespoon of the soy sauce. Refrigerate for a few hours, turning occasionally. Combine the cornflour, vinegar, stock, sugar and remaining soy sauce in a small bowl, stirring to dissolve the cornflour and sugar.

Wearing gloves, cut the tops off the chillies and then roll the chilli between your fingers to squeeze the seeds out. This leaves the chillies whole but because the seeds have been removed, their heat is less intense.

Heat the oil in a wok over high heat. When the oil reaches smoking point, add the chillies and ground pepper and cook for a couple of seconds to release their aroma. Before they begin to burn, add the chicken pieces and stir-fry for 5–6 minutes. Add the capsicum and peanuts and cook for 2 minutes. Add the sauce mixture, pouring it down the side of the wok. Stir-fry for 2–3 minutes, or until the sauce thickens and coats the chicken.

The dominant spice flavour in this dish is star anise, both powdered and whole. The aroma of star anise is quite intoxicating, and its strong, sweet liquorice flavour is perfectly suited to duck and pork dishes.

soy and spice braised duck

1 x 1.9 kg (4 lb 3 oz) duck
2 teaspoons ground star anise
2 teaspoons sea salt flakes
6 thin slices fresh ginger
2 star anise
1 tablespoon peanut oil
2 garlic cloves, peeled
3 tablespoons caster (superfine) sugar
250 ml (9 fl oz/1 cup) dark soy sauce
1 lemon, cut into wedges
1 teaspoon white peppercorns, ground (or 1¼ teaspoons ground white pepper)

Serves 4 as a main

To prepare the duck, remove the fatty parson's nose and surrounding area from the duck to remove the oil glands. Wash and dry the duck and place in a large bowl. Rub the ground star anise and sea salt into the skin, then put the ginger slices and star anise in the duck's cavity. Boil 1 litre (35 fl oz/4 cups) water and set aside.

Heat the oil in a large wok over medium heat. Add the garlic cloves, cook for a few seconds, then add the sugar. Stir quickly to combine, then add the duck. Cook for several minutes, turning constantly with a pair of large kitchen tongs, until the duck is cooked an even brown all over. The oil and sugar mixture gets very hot, so be careful not to burn the duck.

Pour in the hot water and soy sauce and bring to the boil. Reduce the heat to medium, then cover and cook for 2 hours, turning the duck every 30 minutes and basting often with the soy liquid (the duck skin will become quite dark). For the last 30 minutes of cooking, remove the lid to allow most of the liquid to evaporate.

Remove the duck from the wok and allow to cool slightly before cutting into 10–12 smaller pieces. Arrange on a serving platter. Serve with the lemon wedges to squeeze over, and sprinkle with ground white pepper.

Cumin is a common spice ingredient in northern Chinese cooking and is a great flavour with eggplant.

eggplant, cumin and black bean salad

1 teaspoon cumin seeds
2 tablespoons salted black beans, rinsed
2 tablespoons Chinese black vinegar
1 tablespoon light soy sauce
1 teaspoon sesame oil
½ teaspoon caster (superfine) sugar
1 garlic clove, crushed
500 ml (17 fl oz/2 cups) canola or vegetable oil
1 large eggplant (aubergine), about 500 g (1 lb 2 oz), cut into 2 cm (¾ in) cubes
2 ripe tomatoes, cut into 2 cm (¾ in) pieces
2 spring onions (scallions), finely shredded
6–8 coriander (cilantro) sprigs, cut into 3–4 cm (1¼–1½) lengths

Serves 4 as part of a main

Put the cumin seeds in a small frying pan over high heat. Shake the pan over the heat and, when the cumin seeds begin to smoke or crackle, remove from the heat and allow to cool. Use a mortar and pestle to grind the seeds to a rough powder.

To make the dressing, combine the ground cumin, black beans, vinegar, soy sauce, sesame oil, sugar and garlic in a small bowl and stir to dissolve the sugar.

Heat the oil in a wok over high heat. When the surface of the oil is shimmering, add half the eggplant and cook for 2–3 minutes, or until golden. Remove and drain on paper towels. Cook the remaining eggplant. Put the eggplant, tomatoes, spring onions and coriander in a bowl and toss to combine. Arrange on a serving plate and spoon over the dressing.

Strangely enough, the term 'hoisin' translates to mean 'sea-freshness'; in fact, it has a fruity, lightly spiced flavour, which works well in stir-fries. Hoisin can also be thinned down and used as a dipping sauce and it goes particularly well with barbecued meats.

hoisin chicken

1 egg white
1 tablespoon cornflour (cornstarch)
2 tablespoons shaoxing rice wine
850 g (1 lb 14 oz) boneless, skinless chicken thighs, trimmed, each thigh cut into 4 pieces
3 tablespoons hoisin sauce
2 teaspoons light soy sauce
3 tablespoons chicken stock (page 187)
3 tablespoons peanut oil
1 garlic clove, roughly chopped
2 teaspoons grated fresh ginger
4 spring onions (scallions), cut into 3 cm (1¼ in) lengths
1–2 small red chillies, thinly sliced on the diagonal
1 small red capsicum (pepper), julienned

Serves 4 as a main

Put the egg white, cornflour and 1 tablespoon of the rice wine into a small food processor and combine for 1 minute to form a thick, smooth paste. Alternatively, mix the ingredients in a bowl using a small whisk to form a paste. Put the chicken in a non-metallic bowl, add the paste and mix well to coat the chicken in the paste. Refrigerate for a few hours.

Combine the hoisin sauce, soy sauce, stock and remaining rice wine in a bowl.

Heat a wok over high heat and add half the oil, swirling the oil around to coat the wok. Add half the chicken and stir-fry for 5 minutes, or until the chicken is golden brown all over. Repeat with the remaining oil and chicken. Remove the chicken to a plate.

Drain off all but 1 tablespoon of oil from the wok. Add the garlic, ginger, spring onions, chilli and capsicum and stir-fry for 1 minute. Return all the chicken to the wok. Add the sauce mixture, pouring it down the side of the wok, and cook for 2–3 minutes, or until the sauce is thick and syrupy and coats the chicken.

18

sour

高麗蔘

This mild, tangy, no-fuss dressing complements the wonderful natural flavour of an oyster. Because the vinegar is a major flavour component, be sure to use a premium quality brand.

oysters with rice vinegar and salmon roe

1 tablespoon Chinese rice vinegar
2 teaspoons light soy sauce
½ teaspoon caster (superfine) sugar
12 oysters
50 g (1¾ oz) jar salmon roe
1 spring onion (scallion), green part only, very thinly sliced on the diagonal

Serves 2 as a starter

Combine the vinegar, soy sauce and sugar in a small bowl and stir for a few seconds to dissolve the sugar.

Arrange the oysters on a serving plate and divide the roe between the oysters. Sprinkle over some spring onion and drizzle with the dressing.

The tangy, citrus dip used here complements the lightly crumbed prawns.

crumbed prawns with citrus dip

2 tablespoons light soy sauce
1 tablespoon lemon juice
1 tablespoon lime juice
8 raw large prawns (shrimp)
2 tablespoons cornflour (cornstarch)
2 eggs, lightly beaten
120 g (4¼ oz/1½ cups) breadcrumbs, made from day-old bread
canola or vegetable oil, for deep-frying

Serves 4 as a starter

Put the soy sauce and citrus juices in a small bowl and set aside.

Peel the prawns, leaving the tails intact. Cut along the back of each prawn and remove the vein. Open out the prawn a little with your fingers, then place the prawn between two layers of plastic wrap and gently pound with a meat mallet to flatten a little.

Put the cornflour, eggs and breadcrumbs in separate bowls. Toss each prawn in the cornflour, dip into the egg, then gently press into the breadcrumbs, ensuring that each prawn is evenly coated.

Fill a wok one-third full with the oil and heat over medium–high heat. The oil is ready when some breadcrumbs dropped into the wok sizzle on contact with the oil. Add half of the prawns and cook for 2–3 minutes, or until the breadcrumbs turn a dark golden colour. Remove and place on paper towels to drain. Cook the remaining prawns and serve hot with the citrus dip.

The rice vinegar gives this salsa a tangy edge and, with the crispy won tons, is great with a glass of beer or wine.

chinatown salsa with won ton crisps

2 teaspoons chilli flakes
4 Roma (plum) tomatoes
1 small red onion, cut into 5 mm (¼ in) dice
2 tablespoons chopped coriander (cilantro) leaves
1 tablespoon chopped chives
2 tablespoons Chinese rice vinegar
2 teaspoons peanut oil, plus extra for frying
1 teaspoon caster (superfine) sugar
½ teaspoon sea salt flakes
18 round wheat won ton wrappers, cut in half

Serves 4 as a starter

To make the salsa, put the chilli flakes in a dry frying pan over medium heat. Cook until they just begin to smoke, shaking the pan over the heat. Remove from the heat and tip into a bowl. Cut the tomatoes in half and squeeze out most of the seeds. Cut the tomato flesh into 5 mm (¼ in) dice and put in the bowl with the chilli flakes, then add the onion, coriander, chives, vinegar, oil, sugar and sea salt. Gently stir and set aside.

Pour enough oil into a small frying pan to come 1 cm (½ in) up the side of the pan and heat over medium–high heat. The oil is ready when a piece of won ton dropped into the wok sizzles on contact with the oil. Cook the won tons, in two batches, for 1 minute, or until golden, using kitchen tongs to carefully turn them in the oil so they cook evenly. Drain on paper towels. Serve the won ton crisps with the salsa.

Hint: The fried won tons will keep for a couple of days if stored in an airtight container.

INGREDIENTS: V
成份：白酒
NET:60

The dip for these lovely, elegant won tons is simply red vinegar infused with ginger. The Chinese love vinegar and in Chinatown you will see many forms, mostly made from rice but also from wheat bran, grapes or even peaches.

salmon won tons with ginger and red vinegar dip

1 tablespoon finely shredded fresh ginger
3 tablespoons Chinese red vinegar
½ teaspoon caster (superfine) sugar
2 teaspoons cornflour (cornstarch)
200 g (7 oz) skinless salmon fillet
12 square egg won ton wrappers
2 spring onions (scallions), thinly sliced on the diagonal
canola or vegetable oil, for deep-frying

Serves 4 as a starter

To make the dipping sauce, put the ginger in a small heatproof bowl, cover with boiling water and leave to soften for 1 minute. Drain well and put in a small serving bowl along with the vinegar and sugar. Stir to dissolve the sugar, then set aside. Dissolve the cornflour in 2 teaspoons cold water, stirring to form a paste.

Cut the salmon into 1 cm (½ in) wide strips, about 6 cm (2½ in) in length. Put a salmon piece on one side of a won ton wrapper and top with a couple of slices of spring onion. Season with a little salt and black pepper. Brush around the edge of the won ton with some cornflour mixture. Fold the won ton over to enclose the salmon, forming a small rectangle. Press to seal the edges, pressing out any air as you do this. The salmon won tons can be refrigerated until ready to cook.

Fill a wok one-third full with the oil and heat over high heat. When the surface of the oil is shimmering, add half the won tons and cook for about 30 seconds, or until dark golden and crispy. Leave to drain on paper towels while you cook the remaining won tons. Serve with the red vinegar dipping sauce.

Dried noodles often come flavoured with shrimp, scallop or spinach and are sold in clusters called skeins. Spinach noodles are used here, providing colour as well as a lending a wonderful subtle spinach flavour to this tangy, cold noodle dish.

steamed prawns with tangy spinach noodles

2 tablespoons light soy sauce
1 garlic clove, crushed
1 teaspoon finely grated lemon zest
2 tablespoons peanut oil
1 tablespoon Chinese rice vinegar
½ teaspoon caster (superfine) sugar
150 g (5½ oz) dried spinach noodles, about 5 mm (¼ in) wide
16 raw medium prawns (shrimp), peeled and deveined with tails intact
3 spring onions (scallions), thinly sliced on the diagonal
1 small handful chopped coriander (cilantro) leaves

Serves 4 as a starter

To make a dressing, combine the soy sauce, garlic and lemon zest in a small heatproof bowl. Heat the oil in a small saucepan. When the oil reaches smoking point, pour it over the soy sauce mixture and stir to combine. Add the vinegar and sugar to the mixture and stir for a few seconds to dissolve the sugar.

Bring a saucepan of water to the boil and cook the noodles for 5 minutes. Drain and rinse well under cold water.

Bring a wok or large saucepan of water to the boil. Put some baking paper in the bottom of a large bamboo steamer. Prick holes in the paper with a fork or skewer and arrange the prawns in a single layer over the paper. Cover with the lid and steam over boiling water for 3–5 minutes, or until the prawns turn pink.

Put the prawns in a large bowl and pour over the dressing. Add the noodles, spring onions and coriander and toss around to combine and evenly coat the ingredients in the dressing.

This easy-to-make sauce has a good balance of sweet and sour, as well as the most vibrant, natural colour. Be sure to use a Chinese rice vinegar and not white vinegar.

tuna spring rolls with sweet and sour sauce

1 red capsicum (pepper)
3 tablespoons Chinese rice vinegar
55 g (2 oz/¼ cup) caster (superfine) sugar
300 g (10½ oz) fresh tuna fillet, about 2 cm (¾ in) thick
2 teaspoons light soy sauce
12 spring roll wrappers, 12 cm (4½ in) square
canola or vegetable oil, for deep-frying

Serves 4 as a starter

Preheat the oven to 200°C (400°F/Gas 6). Put the capsicum on a lightly oiled baking tray and put into the oven for 20 minutes, turning the capsicum occasionally. Remove from the oven and place in a plastic bag and allow to cool. Peel the capsicum, discarding the skin and seeds. Put the capsicum flesh in a food processor and process for 1 minute, then add 1 tablespoon water, processing until the capsicum is puréed. Strain the puréed capsicum through a fine sieve into a small saucepan. Rub the inside of the sieve with a wooden spoon to remove as much of the liquid as possible. Add the vinegar and sugar to the saucepan and bring to the boil, stirring to dissolve the sugar. Reduce the heat to medium and simmer for 5 minutes, or until the liquid has reduced slightly. Set aside to cool.

Cut the tuna into 12 pieces, each about 1.5 cm (⅝ in) wide and 8 cm (3¼ in) long. Put the tuna in a bowl with the soy sauce, toss to coat in the sauce, then set aside for 10 minutes.

Lay a spring roll wrapper out on a flat surface and rub around the edges with a little water. Put one of the tuna strips in the centre of the wrapper. Fold the end nearest to you over the tuna, fold in the sides and then roll to form a spring roll. Repeat to make 12 rolls in total.

Half-fill a wok with the oil and heat over medium heat. When the surface of the oil is shimmering, add the spring rolls, six at a time, and cook for 20–30 seconds, or until the pastry is crisp and golden. Serve immediately.

Hint: The tuna is cooked rare, but for well-cooked tuna, simply turn the heat down and cook for about 1 minute longer, or until cooked through.

Hot and sour soups are a favourite of mine. The 'sour' comes from the black vinegar—be sure to use a good-quality Chinese black vinegar such as Chinkiang vinegar, which has a full, malty flavour.

hot and sour mushroom soup

4 dried shiitake mushrooms
1 tablespoon vegetable oil
1 teaspoon sesame oil
6 thin slices fresh ginger
100 g (3½ oz) enoki mushrooms, ends trimmed
6 Swiss brown mushrooms
140 g (5 oz) tinned, drained bamboo shoots
1 litre (35 fl oz/4 cups) chicken stock (page 187)
1 tablespoon light soy sauce
2 tablespoons cornflour (cornstarch)
½ teaspoon ground black pepper
½ teaspoon ground white pepper
3 tablespoons Chinese black vinegar
1 tablespoon Chinese rice vinegar

Serves 4 as a starter

Put the shiitake in a bowl, cover with boiling water and soak for 20–30 minutes. Squeeze out the excess liquid from the mushrooms, then remove and discard the stems and cut the caps into thin slices. Reserve 60 ml (2 fl oz/¼ cup) of the soaking liquid.

Heat the vegetable and sesame oils in a saucepan over medium heat and add the ginger, shiitake, enoki and Swiss brown mushrooms and cook for 2–3 minutes, stirring often. Add the bamboo shoots, stock, soy sauce and the reserved mushroom soaking liquid and bring to the boil. Simmer for 5 minutes.

Combine the cornflour with 2 tablespoons water in a small bowl. Add the black and white peppers, and black and rice vinegars to the soup and return to a simmer. Stir in the cornflour mixture and simmer for a couple of minutes, or until the mixture thickens slightly. Serve in small bowls.

Although not traditionally Chinese, this fresh and flavoursome salad can be quickly whipped up using wonderful Chinatown ingredients

tomato and coriander salad

2 tablespoons Chinese rice vinegar
1 tablespoon light soy sauce
1 teaspoon caster (superfine) sugar
1 teaspoon sesame oil
4 tomatoes, cut into large dice
1 Lebanese (short) cucumber, thinly sliced
1 red onion, halved and thinly sliced
1 large handful coriander (cilantro) leaves

Serves 4 as part of a main

To make a dressing, put the vinegar, soy sauce, sugar and sesame oil in a bowl and stir to dissolve the sugar.

Put the tomatoes, cucumber, onion and coriander in a large bowl and gently toss, separating the onion rings. Place on a serving platter and pour over the dressing just before you are ready to serve.

This colourful dish embodies a great stir-fry; it's simple to prepare, quick to cook and has an explosively fresh and tangy flavour.

stir-fry of garlic chives, capsicum and coriander

3 red capsicums (peppers)
100 g (3½ oz/1 bunch) garlic chives
2 teaspoons light soy sauce
1 tablespoon Chinese rice vinegar
¼ teaspoon sea salt flakes
1 tablespoon peanut oil
1 small handful coriander (cilantro) leaves and stems, roughly chopped
1 teaspoon sesame oil

Serves 4 as part of a main

Remove the stalk ends from the capsicums and cut in half. Remove the seeds and carefully run the knife along the inside of the capsicum to remove any of the white membrane. Slice the capsicum into very fine strips. Trim the tough ends from the garlic chives and cut into 4–5 cm (1½–2 in) long pieces.

Combine the soy sauce and vinegar in a small bowl with the sea salt.

Heat a wok over high heat. When the wok is hot, add the oil, swirling the oil around to coat the wok. Add the capsicum and garlic chives and stir-fry for 2 minutes, or until the chives start to become limp and turn dark green. Add the sauce mixture and stir-fry for 1 minute, then briefly stir in the coriander. Turn the heat off and put a lid on the wok. Rest for 1 minute, then stir once more and serve on a plate with the sesame oil drizzled over.

Steaming the chicken before frying it ensures a lovely, golden crispy skin, which is complemented by the tangy, gingery lemon sauce.

lemon chicken

2 boneless chicken breasts, skin on
1 tablespoon vegetable oil
2 tablespoons finely shredded fresh ginger, the length of a matchstick
2 tablespoons shaoxing rice wine
80 ml (2½ fl oz/⅓ cup) lemon juice
2 tablespoons caster (superfine) sugar
1 tablespoon light soy sauce
1 teaspoon sea salt flakes
peanut oil, for frying
2–3 coriander (cilantro) sprigs

Serves 2 as a main

Bring a wok or large saucepan of water to the boil. Put some baking paper in the bottom of a large bamboo steamer. Prick holes in the paper with a fork or skewer and arrange the chicken on top. Cover with a lid and steam over boiling water for 10–15 minutes, or until the chicken is cooked through. Remove the chicken to a plate and refrigerate for at least 6 hours to allow the skin to dry and cool completely.

To make the sauce, heat the vegetable oil in a small saucepan and cook the ginger over medium heat for 20 seconds, long enough for the ginger to wilt slightly, but without allowing it to burn. Add the rice wine and sizzle for 30 seconds. Add the lemon juice, sugar, soy sauce and salt and bring to the boil. Reduce the heat to a low simmer for 8 minutes, or until the sauce thickens slightly.

While the sauce is simmering, heat a wok one-third full of peanut oil over high heat. The oil is hot enough when a cube of bread dropped into the wok sizzles on contact with the oil. Carefully add the chicken, skin side down, and cook for 1 minute. Turn over and cook for 2 minutes. Turn once more to cook, skin side down, for 1 minute, then, finally, skin side up for 1 minute. Remove and allow to cool for a couple of minutes, then slice each chicken breast into five or six pieces. Place the chicken on a deep serving plate, pour over the sauce and garnish with the coriander.

Hint: If you use a chicken breast with the bone in, you will need to steam it for about 20 minutes.

Eggplant is a most versatile vegetable—even though it is a fruit. Usually fried, it can also be steamed, as it is in this recipe. The eggplant's silky, firm flesh readily absorbs the garlicky, mildly sour sauce.

steamed eggplant with vinegar and garlic

1 tablespoon Chinese rice vinegar
2 tablespoons light soy sauce
1 garlic clove, finely chopped
1 teaspoon caster (superfine) sugar
500 g (1 lb 2 oz) eggplant (aubergine)
½–1 large red chilli, to taste, thinly sliced on the diagonal
1 spring onion (scallion), thinly sliced on the diagonal
1 tablespoon peanut oil
1 teaspoon sesame oil

Serves 4 as part of a main

Put the vinegar, soy sauce, garlic and sugar in a small bowl and stir to dissolve the sugar. Set aside. Bring a wok or large saucepan of water to the boil.

Using a mandolin or a sharp knife, slice the eggplant lengthways, as thinly as possible, into ribbons. Place on a serving plate and put the plate into a bamboo steamer. Cover with the lid and put the steamer over the boiling water to steam for 20 minutes. The eggplant should be soft and tender after this time. Carefully remove the plate from the steamer and pour over the sauce. Scatter the chilli and spring onion over the top.

Heat the peanut and sesame oils in a small saucepan until the oil reaches smoking point, then pour the oil over the chilli and spring onion.

This is by no means a traditional Chinese dish. But for a wonderful, easy, summer lunch, all these ingredients can be bought in Chinatown and thrown together without any cooking.

chinatown chicken salad

2 tablespoons light soy sauce
2 tablespoons Chinese rice vinegar
1 teaspoon caster (superfine) sugar
1 teaspoon sesame oil
1 teaspoon grated fresh ginger
1 Chinatown soy chicken, or a barbecued chicken
250 g (9 oz) cherry tomatoes, cut in half
2 large handfuls watercress sprigs
1 handful coriander (cilantro) leaves
3 spring onions (scallions), thinly sliced on the diagonal

Serves 4 as a main

To make the dressing, combine the soy sauce, vinegar, sugar, sesame oil and ginger in a small bowl and add some freshly ground black pepper and a pinch of salt. Stir for a few seconds to dissolve the sugar.

Remove the skin from the chicken and cut the meat into 1 cm (½ in) strips. Put the chicken in a bowl with the tomatoes, watercress, coriander and spring onions and gently toss to combine. Just before serving, drizzle with the dressing.

137

Although the French may argue, no one cooks duck as perfectly as the Chinese. Full of flavour, Chinatown barbecued ducks make an elegant and rich filling for these delicious won tons.

barbecued duck won tons with choy sum

3 tablespoons Chinese red vinegar
2 tablespoons light soy sauce
1 tablespoon shaoxing rice wine
1 teaspoon caster (superfine) sugar
1 teaspoon sesame oil
½ Chinese barbecued duck, skin and flesh finely chopped
1 tablespoon grated fresh ginger
1 garlic clove, crushed
2 spring onions (scallions), chopped
1 tablespoon oyster sauce
1 teaspoon light soy sauce, extra
50 g (1¾ oz/⅓ cup) water chestnuts, roughly chopped
30 round wheat won ton wrappers
2 tablespoons peanut oil
125 ml (4 fl oz/½ cup) chicken stock (page 187)
400 g (14 oz) Chinese flowering cabbage (choy sum), cut into 3 cm (1¼ in) lengths

Serves 4 as a main

Put the vinegar, soy sauce, rice wine and sugar in a bowl and stir to dissolve the sugar. Set aside. Heat a non-stick frying pan over medium heat and add the sesame oil, then add the duck, ginger, garlic and spring onions. Stir-fry for 3–4 minutes. Turn off the heat and add the oyster sauce, extra soy sauce and water chestnuts. Stir to combine, then allow to cool.

Put 1 tablespoon of the cooled mixture in the centre of a won ton wrapper and brush a little water around the edges. Put another won ton wrapper on top, pressing firmly to seal. You should make about 15 won tons, but this may vary depending on the size of the duck.

Heat 1 tablespoon of the peanut oil in a large non-stick frying pan (with a lid) over medium heat and cook half the won tons for 2 minutes, or until lightly golden. Pour in half of the stock. Cover and continue cooking for 2 minutes. Repeat this process to cook the remaining won tons. Meanwhile, bring a large saucepan of water to boil and add the choy sum. Cook for 2–3 minutes, then drain and place on a large serving plate. Put the cooked won tons on the choy sum and serve with the sauce.

This is a traditional recipe made modern with a light beer batter and a crisp and fresh tangy vegetable sauce.

sweet and sour fish

250 ml (9 fl oz/1 cup) chicken stock (page 187)
125 ml (4 fl oz/½ cup) Chinese rice vinegar
80 g (2¾ oz/⅓ cup) caster (superfine) sugar
120 g (4¼ oz/¾ cup) Chinese pickled vegetables
1 tablespoon julienned fresh ginger
1 small carrot, julienned
1 small Lebanese (short) cucumber, seeded and julienned
1 tomato, unripe and almost green, cut into chunks
125 g (4½ oz/1 cup) plain (all-purpose) flour
1 teaspoon baking powder
1 teaspoon sea salt flakes
300 ml (10½ fl oz) cold beer
vegetable or canola oil, for deep-frying
60 g (2¼ oz/½ cup) cornflour (cornstarch)
500 g (1 lb 2 oz) skinless firm white fish fillets, such as John Dory, cut into 4 long strips

Serves 4 as a main

To make the sweet and sour sauce, put the stock, vinegar and sugar in a small saucepan and bring to the boil over high heat. Reduce the heat and bring to a gentle simmer for 20 minutes, or until the sauce has thickened slightly. Stir in the pickles, ginger, carrot, cucumber and tomato and remove from the heat.

To make the batter, combine the flour, baking powder and sea salt in a bowl. Slowly add the beer, constantly beating to form a smooth batter that has the consistency of thick pouring cream.

Half-fill a wok with the oil and heat over medium–high heat. The oil is ready when a teaspoon of the batter dropped into the wok sizzles on contact with the oil. Put the cornflour in a bowl and toss the fish pieces to coat. Dip the fish in the batter, then lower the fish into the oil, cooking them in two batches. Cook for 4–5 minutes, or until dark golden in colour. While the fish is cooking, reheat the sweet and sour sauce over medium heat. Remove the fish from the oil and drain for 1 minute on paper towels. Arrange the fish pieces on a plate and spoon over most of the sauce, reserving some to serve on the side.

sweet

It's the blood oranges that give this dip its exquisite colour. Any other orange will substitute for flavour but not colour. Orange is perfect partnered with a hint of anise. The duck rolls are pretty good too.

duck spring rolls with orange anise dip

250 ml (9 fl oz/1 cup) blood orange juice
55 g (2 oz/¼ cup) caster (superfine) sugar
1 star anise
½ teaspoon chilli flakes
½ Chinese barbecued duck
8 round rice paper wrappers, 22 cm (8½ in) in diameter
1 large handful bean sprouts
80 g (2¾ oz/1 small bunch) garlic chives, cut into 5 cm (2 in) lengths
125 ml (4 fl oz/½ cup) canola or vegetable oil

Serves 4 as a starter

To make the dip, combine the orange juice and sugar in a small saucepan and bring to the boil. Reduce the heat and simmer for 5 minutes, or until slightly thickened. Pour into a bowl and stir in the star anise and chilli flakes. Allow to cool.

Remove the skin and meat from the duck and finely shred both. Soak one rice paper in warm water for 10 seconds and place on a clean tea towel. Repeat with the remaining papers and line them up in a row along the work bench. Divide the duck skin and meat, bean sprouts and garlic chives between the rice papers, placing the ingredients at the end of the wrapper closest to you. Roll over to enclose the mixture, then fold in the sides and continue to roll firmly to enclose the mixture, forming a spring roll.

Heat the oil in a non-stick frying pan over medium–high heat. Add half of the rolls and cook for 2–3 minutes each side, or until lightly golden. Remove and drain on paper towels, then repeat with the remaining spring rolls. Serve with the dipping sauce.

It is very Scandinavian to cure fish in a sugar mixture. A similar technique is used in this recipe, but the addition of soy sauce makes this elegant starter unmistakably Chinese in flavour.

sugar and soy cured tuna

55 g (2 oz/¼ cup) caster (superfine) sugar
125 ml (4 fl oz/½ cup) light soy sauce
2 tablespoons shaoxing rice wine
250 g (9 oz) sashimi-quality tuna steak, 2–3 cm (¾–1¼ in) thick
1 small handful watercress sprigs
2 spring onions (scallions), thinly sliced on the diagonal
1 teaspoon sesame oil

Serves 4 as a starter

Combine the sugar, soy sauce and rice wine in a small non-metallic dish (the dish should be small enough so that the tuna fits snugly), stirring until the sugar has dissolved. Add the tuna, turning to coat in the marinade, then put into the refrigerator and marinate for 24 hours, turning the fish over after 12 hours.

Drain the tuna from the marinade and thinly slice across the grain. Scatter the watercress over a serving plate, arrange the tuna over the top and garnish with the spring onions. Drizzle over the sesame oil to serve.

I don't need an excuse to eat these versatile pancakes. Here they are wrapped around a sweet and colourful stir-fry of honey beef and carrot.

honey beef in peking pancakes

300 g (10½ oz) beef fillet, trimmed
1 teaspoon cornflour (cornstarch)
1 tablespoon shaoxing rice wine
2 tablespoons light soy sauce
8–10 peking duck (mandarin) pancakes
500 ml (17 fl oz/2 cups) peanut oil
2 garlic cloves, finely chopped
1 carrot, julienned
2 tablespoons honey
2 teaspoons sesame seeds, toasted
1 teaspoon chilli flakes

Serves 4 as a starter

Put the beef fillet in the freezer for a few hours until firm. Thinly slice the fillet into 5 mm (¼ in) thick slices, then slice across the grain into thin matchsticks. Put the beef in a non-metallic bowl with the cornflour, rice wine and 1 tablespoon of the soy sauce and toss around to evenly coat the beef in the marinade. Refrigerate for a few hours.

Preheat the oven to 160°C (315°F/Gas 2–3). Wrap the pancakes in foil and warm in the oven for 10 minutes.

Heat the oil in a wok over high heat. The oil is ready when a slice of beef dropped into the wok sizzles on contact with the oil and then floats to the surface. Add half the beef slices and cook for 1 minute. Remove and drain on paper towels. Repeat with the remaining beef.

Drain all but 1 tablespoon of oil from the wok. Add the garlic and carrot and stir-fry for 1 minute over high heat. Return the beef to the wok, then add the honey and remaining soy sauce and stir-fry for 2–3 minutes, or until the liquid has almost evaporated and has thickened and darkened in colour.

Combine the sesame seeds and chilli flakes in a small serving bowl. Put the honey beef in a separate bowl and serve the pancakes and sesame mixture on the side. To serve, place some beef in the pancake, sprinkle with the sesame and chilli flakes and roll up to eat.

Honey prawns are an iconic item in Australian–Chinese restaurants. Using oyster sauce in the batter is a trick of my dad's. It seasons the batter while also providing a golden effect when cooked.

honey prawns

60 g (2¼ oz/½ cup) plain (all-purpose) flour
60 g (2¼ oz/½ cup) cornflour (cornstarch), plus 2 extra tablespoons
1 egg, lightly beaten
1 tablespoon oyster sauce
125 ml (4 fl oz/½ cup) cold beer
vegetable or canola oil, for deep-frying
12 raw large prawns (shrimp), peeled and deveined with tails intact
115 g (4 oz/⅓ cup) honey
1 tablespoon sesame seeds, toasted

Serves 4 as part of a main

Combine the flour, cornflour and a pinch of salt in a bowl. Make a well in the centre and, using a fork or chopsticks, beat in the egg, oyster sauce and beer to form a thick batter that has the consistency of thick pouring cream.

Half-fill a wok with the oil and heat over medium–high heat. The oil is hot enough when the surface starts to shimmer. Put the extra cornflour in a bowl. Dip the prawns in the cornflour, shaking off any excess and set aside. Dip half of the prawns in the batter, then carefully lower the prawns into the hot oil using kitchen tongs. Cook for 3–4 minutes, or until the prawns are light golden and crispy, turning them around in the oil to evenly cook. Remove and place on paper towels to drain. Repeat with the remaining prawns.

Put the honey in a small saucepan over medium heat and bring just to sizzling point. Place the prawns on a serving platter and pour over the honey. Sprinkle over the sesame seeds and serve immediately.

Char siu is Chinatown barbecued pork. The slightly sweet, slightly spicy flavour of the marinade used for the barbecued pork—which gives it its distinctive red glaze—is also excellent with lamb. The flavours of the sauce, when combined with a few other fresh flavours, turn this simple rack of lamb into a knock-out roast.

char siu rack of lamb

80 ml (2½ fl oz/⅓ cup) Chinese barbecue (char siu) sauce
2 tablespoons honey
80 ml (2½ fl oz/⅓ cup) lemon juice
1 teaspoon sesame oil
2 x 375 g (13 oz) racks of lamb
1 tablespoon peanut oil

Serves 4 as a main

Combine the barbecue sauce, honey, lemon juice and sesame oil. Put the racks in a large non-metallic dish and pour over the marinade. Using your hands, rub the marinade evenly all over the lamb. Put in the refrigerator and allow to marinate for at least 8 hours.

Preheat the oven to 220°C (425°F/Gas 7). Heat the oil in a large frying pan and add the lamb racks. Cook over medium–high heat for about 30 seconds on each side, turning the lamb just as it begins to burn a little. This will help give it that slight char siu flavour. Transfer the lamb to a roasting tin and put into the oven for 20 minutes. Remove the lamb from the oven and rest the meat for 5 minutes, then slice either into individual cutlets or serve whole to carve at the table.

Here the veal shin is made sweet and unctuous by slow cooking with dark soy sauce and rock sugar.

chinatown osso bucco with orange

4 x 200 g (7 oz) pieces of osso bucco
3 tablespoons mushroom oyster sauce
1 tablespoon vegetable oil
2 garlic cloves, roughly chopped
2 teaspoons grated fresh ginger
80 ml (2½ fl oz/⅓ cup) shaoxing rice wine
1 litre (35 fl oz/4 cups) chicken stock
1 tablespoon dark soy sauce
70 g (2½ oz) yellow rock sugar
3 pieces dried orange peel
3 slivers fresh orange peel
1 teaspoon finely grated orange zest
2 tablespoons roughly chopped coriander (cilantro) leaves
½ teaspoon ground white pepper

Serves 4 as a main

Preheat the oven to 180°C (350°F/Gas 4). Put the osso bucco in a bowl with the mushroom oyster sauce and rub the sauce over the meat to coat.

Heat the oil in a heavy-based flameproof casserole dish over medium heat. Cook the meat for 2 minutes each side to seal it, then remove from the pan. Add the garlic and ginger and cook for 1 minute, stirring constantly. Add the rice wine and sizzle for 1 minute, scraping up any sediment on the bottom of the dish. Return the meat to the dish and add the stock, soy sauce, rock sugar, and dried and fresh orange peel and stir to combine the ingredients, scraping the bottom of the dish to remove any sediment.

Put the casserole dish in the oven and cook for 1 hour, then remove from the oven and turn the meat over, giving it a good stir. Return to the oven and cook for a further 1 hour, or until the meat is very tender and beginning to fall off the bone. Remove the meat to a serving plate and place the casserole dish on the stovetop. Bring the sauce to the boil and cook for 8 minutes, or until the sauce has reduced and thickened. Pour over the osso bucco and serve sprinkled with the orange zest, coriander and pepper.

Sweet and sour does not have to mean thick and gluggy. This sweet and sour is light, crisp and fresh, with the pineapple making it a little bit tropical.

sweet and sour pork

600 g (1 lb 5 oz) pork neck
30 g (1 oz/¼ cup) cornflour (cornstarch)
2 egg yolks, lightly beaten
1 tablespoon oyster sauce
170 g (6 oz/¾ cup) caster (superfine) sugar
1 star anise
1 tablespoon finely shredded fresh ginger
100 g (3½ oz) fresh pineapple, cut into small wedges
1 firm, unripe tomato, cut into thin wedges
40 g (1½ oz/¼ cup) Chinese pickled vegetables
750 ml (26 fl oz/3 cups) canola or vegetable oil
60 g (2¼ oz/½ cup) plain (all-purpose) flour
1 Lebanese (short) cucumber, seeded, thinly sliced
1 red chilli, julienned

Serves 4 as a main

Slice the pork across the grain into 5 mm (¼ in) thick pieces, then slice into 1 cm (½ in) wide strips. Put 1½ tablespoons of the cornflour in a large bowl with 1 tablespoon cold water and mix to a paste. Add the egg yolks and oyster sauce and mix to combine. Add the pork and toss to coat in the marinade, then refrigerate for a few hours.

Combine the sugar, star anise and ginger with 185 ml (6 fl oz/¾ cup) cold water in a saucepan and bring to the boil for 10–12 minutes. Add the pineapple, tomato and pickles and cook over medium heat for 10–12 minutes, or until the sauce is quite syrupy. Set aside.

Heat the oil in a wok over high heat. Meanwhile, add the plain flour and the remaining cornflour to the pork and use your hands to combine. Test the heat of the oil by frying a piece of pork. It is ready when a piece of pork dropped into the wok sizzles on contact with the hot oil. Add one-third of the pork and cook for 1 minute, or until the pork is light golden and crispy. Remove and drain on paper towels. Repeat until all the pork is cooked.

Allow the oil to reheat, then return all the pork to the wok and cook for 2–3 minutes, or until dark golden. Drain on paper towels and arrange on a serving plate. Reheat the sauce for a few minutes and serve with the pork. Scatter the cucumber and chilli over the top.

綬帶來信

Twice cooking the duck produces a crispy skin and succulent flesh, which goes beautifully with the spicy, fruity sauce. Mandarins are used here, but fruit such as sweet oranges, blood oranges or plums also work very well.

mandarin and sweet spiced duck

1 teaspoon Chinese five-spice
2 x 300 g (10½ oz) duck breasts, leg attached, skin on
2 mandarins
170 g (6 oz/¾ cup) caster (superfine) sugar
3 star anise
1 cinnamon stick
1 tablespoon light soy sauce
1 teaspoon Chinese rice vinegar
500 ml (17 fl oz/2 cups) canola or vegetable oil

Serves 4 as a main

Bring a wok or large saucepan of water to the boil. Rub the five-spice over the duck pieces. Put some baking paper in the bottom of a large bamboo steamer. Prick holes in the paper with a fork or skewer and arrange the duck on top. Cover with the lid and steam over the boiling water for 20 minutes. Remove the duck from the steamer, put on a plate and refrigerate, uncovered, for 3 hours or until completely cooled, or preferably overnight.

Remove the skin and pith from the mandarins, reserving 2 thick strips of peel. Cut the mandarins in half crossways. Combine the sugar with 185 ml (6 fl oz/¾ cup) water in a large saucepan and bring the mixture to the boil for 5 minutes, stirring often. Add the mandarin halves, star anise and cinnamon stick, along with the reserved strips of peel, and cook for a further 2 minutes. Stir in the soy sauce and vinegar, then remove from the heat.

Heat the oil in a wok over high heat. When the surface of the oil is shimmering, lower the duck into the oil, skin side down. Cook for 2 minutes, turn the duck and cook for another 2 minutes. Repeat this again, cooking for a further 2 minutes each side. Put the duck onto a chopping board to rest for 5 minutes. Cut the breast into thick slices and arrange on the serving plate along with the duck leg and mandarin halves. Spoon over the mandarin sauce and spices.

Hint: If you can't find duck breasts with the leg attached, buy two large breasts with the bone in and skin on.

159

Rock sugar, a stunning and exotic looking ingredient, is appropriately named as it comes as uneven, large lumps of sugar. It is combined here with maltose, a barley-based sweetener, to add a dark caramel glaze to the salmon.

sweet soy-glazed salmon

50 g (1¾ oz) yellow rock sugar
1 tablespoon maltose
125 ml (4 fl oz/½ cup) light soy sauce
500 g (1 lb 2 oz) salmon fillet, skin on
1 teaspoon peanut oil
1 teaspoon sesame seeds
½ teaspoon ground sichuan peppercorns (optional)

Serves 4 as part of a main

Crush the sugar using a mortar and pestle, then put the sugar in a small saucepan. Add the maltose, soy sauce and 60 ml (2 fl oz/¼ cup) water. Bring the mixture to the boil, then reduce the heat to a simmer for 5 minutes, stirring often to dissolve the sugar. Set aside and allow the mixture to cool. Put the cooled soy mixture in a bowl and add the salmon. Toss the salmon around in the mixture to evenly coat.

Preheat the oven to 200°C (400°F/Gas 6). Heat the oil in a non-stick frying pan over medium heat and cook the salmon, skin side up, for 1 minute, taking care not to burn the fish. Turn over and cook for 1 minute on the skin side. Place the salmon in a roasting tin and put into the oven for 6–8 minutes, or until cooked through. Serve sprinkled with the sesame seeds and ground pepper, if using. Serve with a cucumber salad (page 103).

Sweet pickled vegetables come in a variety of guises—look for mixed vegetables in a thick syrup. Serve this dish with rice to offset the sweetness.

pork with orange and sweet pickles

500 g (1 lb 2 oz) pork fillet
1 teaspoon cornflour (cornstarch)
1 tablespoon light soy sauce
1 tablespoon shaoxing rice wine
1 tablespoon caster (superfine) sugar
1 teaspoon Chinese rice vinegar
250 ml (9 fl oz/1 cup) peanut oil
1 garlic clove, roughly chopped
2 teaspoons grated fresh ginger
2 spring onions (scallions), finely chopped
1 small red chilli, seeded and finely chopped
170 g (6 oz/1 cup) Chinese sweet pickles, roughly chopped
1 teaspoon finely grated orange zest

Serves 4 as a main

Put the pork fillet in the freezer for 2–3 hours, or until firm. Thinly slice the pork into 5 mm (1/4 in) thick slices, then slice across the grain into thin matchsticks. Put the pork strips in a non-metallic bowl with the cornflour, half of the soy sauce and half of the rice wine. Toss in the bowl to coat in the marinade, then refrigerate for at least 1 hour.

Put the sugar, vinegar, remaining soy sauce and remaining rice wine in a small bowl and stir to combine. Set aside.

Heat the oil in a wok over high heat. When the surface of the oil is shimmering, add the pork strips in batches and cook for 1 minute, stirring and separating them as they cook. Remove and drain on paper towels.

Remove all but 2 tablespoons of oil from the wok. Add the garlic, ginger, spring onions and chilli to the wok and stir-fry over high heat for a few seconds. Add the sweet pickles and orange zest and cook for 1 minute. Return the pork to the wok and stir-fry for 2 minutes, then pour in the sauce mixture. Cook for 2 minutes, tossing all the ingredients around to evenly combine.

At Chinese restaurants you will often see 'eggplant in special sauce' on the menu. No one seems to agree on what makes that sauce so special. This is my special version.

eggplant in special sauce

1 tablespoon ground bean sauce
1 tablespoon hoisin sauce
1 tablespoon caster (superfine) sugar
500 ml (17 fl oz/2 cups) canola or vegetable oil
1 large eggplant (aubergine), about 425 g (15 oz), cut into 3 cm (1¼ in) cubes
1 teaspoon sesame oil
1 garlic clove, chopped
2 spring onions (scallions), white part chopped, green part thinly sliced on the diagonal
2 teaspoons grated fresh ginger

Serves 4 as part of a main

Put the bean sauce, hoisin sauce, sugar and 3 tablespoons water in a small bowl and stir to combine.

Heat the oil in a wok over high heat. When the surface of the oil is shimmering, carefully add the eggplant and cook for 3–4 minutes, or until the eggplant begins to turn golden. Remove and drain on paper towels.

Drain all but 1 teaspoon of the oil from the wok. Add the sesame oil, garlic, the white part of the spring onion and ginger and cook over high heat for 10 seconds, or until aromatic, taking care that they don't burn. Add the sauce mixture and bring to the boil for 3 minutes, or until the sauce begins to thicken and become syrupy. Return the eggplant to the wok and cook for 1 minute, turning the eggplant carefully to avoid breaking it up. Serve with the spring onion greens scattered over the top.

Fresh fruit is commonly served at the end of a Chinese meal. Coating the fruit in a light toffee is an exotic alternative and works very well not only with figs but also with strawberries, apple slices and pineapple.

chinatown toffeed figs

400 g (14 oz) yellow rock sugar
1 teaspoon Chinese rice vinegar
8 large figs, stems intact

Serves 4 as a light dessert

Crush the sugar using a mortar and pestle, then put the sugar in a small saucepan. Add 250 ml (9 fl oz/1 cup) water and the vinegar and cook over low heat, stirring often, until the sugar has completely dissolved. Put a candy thermometer in the saucepan and increase the heat to medium. Bring the mixture to the boil, without stirring. Brush the side of the saucepan with a little cold water to stop the toffee from burning around the edges. Cook until the temperature reaches 150–155°C (300°F), or hard crack stage. Take care as the toffee darkens very quickly once it reaches this point.

If you don't have a candy thermometer, test that the toffee has reached the correct stage by using a teaspoon to drop some of the hot syrup into a saucer of cold water—the toffee should form a hard ball that can be stretched and snapped.

Remove the toffee from the heat. Using a pair of kitchen tongs, hold the fig by the stem and dip it into the toffee in the pan for a few seconds, rolling it around in the toffee to evenly coat. Remove and place on some greaseproof paper. Repeat with the remaining figs. Allow to cool, then serve within a few hours.

This Chinatown bombe Alaska makes use of soft sponge cakes, sold in bakeries and often called 'sally cakes'.

fried ice cream with butterscotch sauce

8 scoops vanilla ice cream, about 3–4 cm (1¼–1½ in) in diameter
1 egg, lightly beaten
300 g (10½ oz) pound (Madeira) or plain sponge cake, cut into 5 mm (¼ in) thick slices
125 g (4½ oz) unsalted butter
90 g (3¼ oz/½ cup) lightly packed soft brown sugar
125 ml (4 fl oz/½ cup) cream (whipping)
canola or vegetable oil, for deep-frying

Serves 4

Line a tray with baking paper. Put the ice cream balls on the tray and then put into the freezer until the ice cream is hard.

Brush a little of the egg onto one side of the cake slices and wrap around the ice cream balls, egg side in, totally enclosing the ice cream in cake. Roll the caked ice cream balls in your hand to create an even ball shape and place on the tray and into the freezer overnight.

To make the butterscotch sauce, put the butter and brown sugar in a small saucepan and cook over low heat until the butter has melted. Stir to combine, then gradually pour in the cream. Stir over low heat for 4–5 minutes. Remove from the heat.

Fill a wok one-third full with the oil and heat over high heat. When the surface of the oil is shimmering, add an ice cream ball and cook for a few seconds (the cake mixture will cook very quickly). Put into a serving bowl and repeat with the other ice cream balls, cooking one at a time. Serve two ice cream balls per person and serve with the butterscotch sauce to pour over the top.

An icy, fruit sorbet helps to cleanse the palate between courses, or is a perfect ending to a meal.

mandarin sorbet

230 g (8 oz/1 cup) caster (superfine) sugar
500 ml (17 fl oz/2 cups) fresh mandarin juice
1 egg white

Serves 4

Put the sugar and 250 ml (9 fl oz/1 cup) water in a small saucepan and bring to the boil, stirring often. Reduce the heat and simmer for 5 minutes. Allow the mixture to cool completely. Put the sugar syrup and mandarin juice in an ice-cream machine and churn until almost frozen.

Lightly beat the egg white until soft peaks form and add to the partially frozen sorbet. Churn for a further 5–10 minutes to combine. Put into a container and freeze until set.

Alternatively, if you don't have an ice-cream machine, put the sugar syrup and mandarin juice in a bowl. Stir to combine, then put into the freezer, stirring every couple of hours, until set firm. Remove and cut into blocks and put in a food processor. Beat the egg white until soft peaks form and add to the sorbet in the food processor and process for 1 minute. Return to the freezer until set.

Hint: You will need about 8–10 mandarins to obtain 500 ml (17 fl oz/2 cups) juice, although this will depend on the size of fruit. Juice a mandarin as you would an orange. Cut the mandarin in half crossways and juice using a citrus juicer. Strain into a bowl.

The subtlety of jasmine tea works really well as an ice cream flavour. However, the quality of tea can vary greatly, so use your nose and choose a brand that is heady with the fragrance of jasmine flower.

jasmine tea ice cream

20 g (¾ oz) good-quality jasmine tea leaves (3 tablespoons)
230 g (8 oz/1 cup) caster (superfine) sugar
500 ml (17 fl oz/2 cups) cream (whipping)
3 egg yolks, lightly beaten in a heatproof bowl

Serves 4

Put the jasmine tea leaves in a heatproof bowl and pour over 250 ml (9 fl oz/1 cup) boiling water. Allow to infuse for 5 minutes, then strain into a bowl. Discard the leaves and allow the tea to cool.

Put the sugar and 250 ml (9 fl oz/1 cup) of the cream in a small saucepan over low heat and cook for 5 minutes, stirring occasionally, until the sugar dissolves. Remove from the heat and gradually whisk this mixture into the eggs, mixing well to combine. Pour the custard back into a clean saucepan and cook over low heat for 8–10 minutes, stirring constantly, or until the mixture thickens and coats the back of the spoon. Put in a bowl and allow to cool, stirring regularly to prevent a skin forming.

Combine the tea, custard mixture and remaining cream in an ice-cream machine and churn according to the manufacturer's instructions. If you don't have an ice-cream machine, pour the mixture into a shallow metal tin and freeze for 2 hours. Remove from the freezer and, working quickly, transfer the mixture to a large bowl and beat with electric beaters until smooth. Pour the mixture back into the tray and refreeze. Repeat this step three times. For the final freezing, place in an airtight container and cover the surface with a piece of greaseproof paper. Serve the ice cream with some fresh fruit.

I have made up my own five-spice mixture here, using whole spices—the exotic combination gives a wonderful deep, rich flavour to this dish. I've used plumcots, a hybrid of a plum and apricot, although you could substitute any stone fruit.

five-spiced plumcots

450 g (1 lb/2 cups) caster (superfine) sugar
1 cinnamon stick
1 star anise
1 cardamom pod
6–8 fennel seeds
6 sichuan peppercorns
1 tablespoon lemon juice
8 plumcots

Serves 4

Put the sugar in a heavy-based saucepan with the cinnamon stick, star anise, cardamom, fennel seeds, peppercorns, lemon juice and 1 litre (35 fl oz/4 cups) water. Bring to the boil, then add the plumcots. Reduce the heat to low and simmer for 30 minutes, or until the fruit is soft.

Remove the plumcots from the poaching syrup, reserving the syrup. When the plumcots are cool enough to handle, peel them and place in a serving bowl. Serve the plumcots warm or at room temperature with the syrup poured over them.

You will find dried liquorice root near the other exotic smelling ingredients like star anise and cinnamon. Just follow your nose...

fruit salad with spiced lime syrup

115 g (4 oz/½ cup) caster (superfine) sugar
12 thin slices dried liquorice root
2 star anise
1 tablespoon lime juice
200 g (7 oz) cherries, stems attached
550 g (1 lb 4 oz) tinned lychees, drained
vanilla ice cream, to serve (optional)

Serves 4

Put the sugar, liquorice root and star anise in a small saucepan with 250 ml (9 fl oz/1 cup) water. Bring to the boil, then reduce the heat to low and simmer for 12–15 minutes, or until the liquid has reduced slightly to form a syrup. Allow to cool, then stir in the lime juice.

Put the fruit in individual serving bowls and drizzle with the spiced syrup. Serve with vanilla ice cream, if desired.

Hint: If fresh lychees are in season, substitute the tinned version with 225 g (8 oz) peeled fresh lychees. When draining the tinned lychees, reserve the syrup to make Lychee delight (page 184).

LICHT GEZOET

567 GRAM

S. (567 GRAM

At the end of a Chinese meal it is usual to be presented with a plate of fresh fruit or biscuits. However, these Chinatown biscotti can be eaten at any time of day. Serve with a fragrant cup of jasmine or green tea.

orange, almond and fennel seed biscuits

80 g (2¾ oz) unsalted butter, softened
170 g (6 oz/¾ cup) caster (superfine) sugar
½ teaspoon fennel seeds
2 teaspoons grated orange zest
2 eggs
250 g (9 oz/2 cups) plain (all-purpose) flour
1 teaspoon baking powder
80 g (2¾ oz/½ cup) blanched almonds, lightly toasted and roughly chopped

Makes about 40

Preheat the oven to 180°C (350°F/Gas 4). Line a baking tray with baking paper.

Put the butter, sugar, fennel seeds and orange zest in a food processor and combine for 1 minute. Add the eggs and combine until smooth, then add the flour and baking powder and combine. Depending on the size of the food processor, you may need to do this in two batches.

Put the dough on a lightly floured board and knead in the almonds for about 2 minutes, or until the almonds are evenly incorporated and the mixture forms into one ball.

Separate the dough into two equal portions and roughly form each into a log about 20 cm (8 in) long and 4–5 cm (1½–2 in) wide. Put the logs on the baking tray and into the oven for 25 minutes. Remove and allow to cool for a few minutes. Reduce the oven temperature to 170°C (325°F/Gas 3). Carefully cut the logs into 1 cm (½ in) thick slices. Put half of the biscuit slices back onto the baking tray, in a single layer, and return to the oven. Bake for 10 minutes, then turn the biscuits over and bake for a further 10 minutes, or until golden brown. Repeat with the remaining slices. Allow to cool completely before serving. Serve with tea and fresh fruit, such as stone fruit, orange or grapes. Store in an airtight container.

These crisp, buttery almond cookies are a perfect treat with fragrant jasmine tea.

almond cookies

250 g (9 oz) unsalted butter, softened
230 g (8 oz/1 cup) caster (superfine) sugar
1 egg, lightly beaten
300 g (10½ oz/2½ cups) plain (all-purpose) flour
1½ teaspoons baking powder
48 blanched almonds

Makes 48

Using electric beaters, cream the butter and sugar for 5 minutes, or until pale and creamy. Add the egg, beating for 1 minute, then fold in the flour and baking powder. Form the mixture into one large ball, then divide into four. Put the dough portions on a lightly floured board and roll each into a log about 12 cm (4½ in) long. Firmly wrap each log in plastic wrap and refrigerate for about 1 hour, or until firm enough to slice.

Preheat the oven to 200°C (400°F/Gas 6). Line a baking tray with baking paper.

Cut 1 cm (½ in) thick rounds from the logs and arrange on the baking tray. Firmly press an almond into the centre of each and bake for 18–20 minutes, or until golden. Remove to a wire rack to cool. Store in an airtight container.

Stem ginger preserved in syrup can be bought in Chinatown in decorative ceramic pots. The gingery flavour here is quite subtle, although you may notice that its flavour does intensify after a few days.

mum's ginger and almond slice

175 g (6 oz) unsalted butter, softened
230 g (8 oz/1 cup) caster (superfine) sugar
1 egg, lightly beaten
225 g (8 oz/1¾ cups) plain (all-purpose) flour
125 g (4½ oz) ginger in syrup, finely chopped
70 g (2½ oz/¾ cup) flaked almonds
1 tablespoon milk
1 tablespoon sugar

Makes about 26 pieces

Preheat the oven to 180°C (350°F/Gas 4). Line and lightly grease a 20 x 30 x 4 cm (8 x 12 x 1½ in) baking tin.

Using electric beaters, cream the butter and sugar for 2–3 minutes, or until pale and creamy. Add the egg and beat for 1 minute. Stir in the flour, ginger and half the almonds. The mixture will be quite dry. Put the mixture into the tin and gently press to fit in the tin. Brush the top with the milk and sprinkle over the remaining almonds and the sugar. Bake for 50 minutes. Allow to cool, then cut in half across the length, then into fingers, each about 2 cm (¾ in) wide. This slice will keep for several days in the refrigerator.

Hint: If ginger in syrup is unavailable, substitute glacé ginger.

The simplicity and uniqueness of the flavour of lychee is encapsulated in this colourful and palate-refreshing delight.

lychee delight

750 ml (26 fl oz/3 cups) lychee syrup, from tinned lychees
220 g (7¾ oz/1 cup) sugar
125 g (4½ oz/1 cup) cornflour (cornstarch)
1 teaspoon cream of tartar
pink food colouring
2 tablespoons icing (confectioner's) sugar
2 tablespoons cornflour (cornstarch), extra

Serves 4

Line a 20 x 30 x 4 cm (8 x 12 x 1½ in) baking tin with plastic wrap.

Bring the lychee syrup to boil in a large, heavy-based saucepan. Add the sugar and stir until dissolved. Remove from the heat.

Combine the cornflour, cream of tartar and 250 ml (9 fl oz/1 cup) cold water in a bowl. Gradually add this to the syrup. Return the saucepan to medium heat and stir until the mixture boils. Reduce the heat to low and cook for 40 minutes, stirring frequently. The mixture will thicken and become clear. Add a couple of drops of food colouring and stir well. Pour the mixture into the tray and leave to set for 4–6 hours.

Combine the icing sugar and extra cornflour in a bowl. Before serving, cut the set mixture into 3–4 cm (1¼–1½ in) squares and dip one side of the square into the icing sugar mixture.

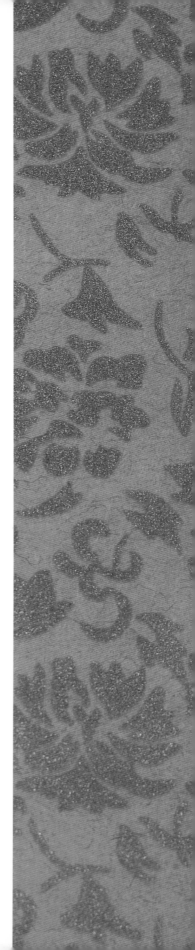

basic recipes

chicken stock

1 large chicken, about 1.8–2 kg (4 lb–4 lb 8 oz)
4–6 thin slices fresh ginger
4–6 spring onions (scallions), each cut into 4 pieces

Trim any excess fat from the chicken. Wash the chicken well and dry with paper towels. Cut the chicken into 8–10 pieces and place in a large saucepan with the ginger slices and spring onions. Pour over 3 litres (105 fl oz/12 cups) water and bring to the boil. Reduce the heat to low and gently simmer the stock for 2 hours, skimming the surface of the stock to remove any debris or impurities. Remove from the heat and strain through a fine sieve or through muslin (cheesecloth). Use the fresh stock within 3 days, or freeze until needed.

sichuan pepper and salt mixture

1 tablespoon sichuan peppercorns
2 teaspoons white peppercorns
2 tablespoons salt

Put the sichuan peppercorns, white peppercorns and salt in a dry frying pan and cook over high heat until the peppercorns start to smoke or pop and the salt darkens in colour. Remove and allow to cool, then grind to a powder using either a spice mill or mortar and pestle.

Use the amount of mixture specified for each recipe and store any unused mixture in an airtight container. Makes 2 tablespoons.

glossary

bamboo shoots Soft shoots of bamboo, ivory coloured and conical in shape. The shoots are sold whole or presliced in tins.

black vinegar Chinese black vinegar is an aged vinegar, dark brown in colour and with a complex tangy and malty flavour. Those from Chinkiang are very good. It is similar, but more subtle in flavour, to balsamic vinegar.

canola oil This golden-coloured, odourless oil is excellent for deep-frying.

chicken stock A light-coloured, almost clear broth made by slow poaching chicken in water with ginger and spring onions (scallions). Used in soups, stir-fries, steamed and slow-braised dishes. Home-made chicken stock can be frozen in small quantities for later use. Most commercial brands have overpowering flavour additives, but the best ready-made brand is Swanson, sold in tins and cartons, in the Asian section of most supermarkets.

chilli sauce Fiery, red, thick sauce made from chilli, vinegar, sugar and salt. Often used as a dipping sauce and is also a spicy addition to stir-fries. Use a Chinese brand such as Koon Yick Wah Kee.

chilli–garlic sauce Made from garlic, chilli and vinegar. An excellent condiment and base for stir-fries.

Chinese pickled vegetables
A colourful mixture of vegetables in a clear vinegar, used to give colour and texture to stir-fries.

Chinese sweet pickles Mixed shredded vegetables in a thick, syrupy sugar-based liquid. They are used to flavour sweet stir-fried dishes.

cinnamon sticks Curled, woody bark of the cinnamon tree used to add intense flavour to braised dishes, and an essential flavour component of five-spice.

dried chillies These come in a variety of sizes, with the smaller generally being hotter in flavour. Dried chillies impart a smoky flavour to dishes.

dried orange peel Intensely flavoured dried skin of oranges or tangerines, used to flavour braises.

dry-roasting To dry-roast cashews or peanuts, put the nuts in a frying pan over low heat, stirring regularly, or until the nuts are lightly golden. Alternatively, put the nuts in a 180°C (350°F/Gas 4) oven and roast for 8–10 minutes, until golden.

egg noodles Long egg noodles are the noodles used in 'long' soup. Dried, these noodles are sold in clusters called 'skeins'. They are also sold fresh and should be stored in the refrigerator.

five-spice A Chinese mixed spice, generally made with star anise, fennel seeds, sichuan peppercorns, cinnamon and cloves.

ginger in syrup This candied young ginger, sometimes called stem ginger, is preserved in a thick, sweet syrup.

ground bean sauce An intensely flavoured, thick, brown paste made from ground, salted soya beans.

hoisin sauce This sauce, made from ground soya beans, sugar and spices, goes very well with barbecued meats.

jasmine tea leaves This tea can vary greatly in quality—buy tea with a strong fragrance. The tea has small, twisted leaves and dried flower buds.

lap cheong Sweet, dried pork sausages, generally sold in packets, each containing 10–12 sausages, about 10 cm (4 in) in length. Cook to soften before eating, either by steaming or stir-frying.

maltose This thick sweetener is made from barley and is incredibly sticky. Heating a spoon under boiling water will make it easier to remove from its container.

mushroom soy sauce Flavoured with straw mushrooms, this soy-based sauce falls between light and dark soy sauce in colour and consistency. It is a flavoursome seasoning alternative for stir-fried and steamed dishes.

oyster sauce A thick, brown, lightly caramel flavoured sauce made from oyster extract and soy sauce. Mushroom oyster sauce is slightly darker with a rich flavour, given by the addition of mushrooms. Lee Kum Kee is a recommended brand.

peking duck pancakes
Sometimes called mandarin pancakes, these are sold fresh or frozen in Chinatown, or in restaurants that sell barbecued ducks and meat. Steam to soften before eating.

peanut oil Dark golden peanut oil has a strong peanutty aroma and is best used in small amounts in stir-fries. The lighter coloured, golden peanut oil is lighter in flavour and used in this book. It is good for frying, as it can be heated to high temperatures without burning.

red vinegar Chinese red vinegar is ideal for use in dips and cold sauces.

rice noodles Fresh, white and slightly oily noodles made from rice and water. Sold in slabs or precut into widths ready to be used in stir-fries and soups.

rice stick noodles Made from rice flour, these clear and brittle noodles range in width. Soak in water prior to cooking, which will turn them white.

rice vinegar Made from distilled rice, Chinese vinegars are milder than Western ones. They are generally clear or light golden in colour.

salted black beans Also known as dried, fermented soya beans. These soft, flavoursome beans go well with garlic, ginger and chilli. Often rinsed before use, although this isn't always necessary.

sesame oil Golden brown with a strong, rich flavour, sesame oil gives flavour to stir-fries, soups, sauces and dressings. It is only used sparingly because of its strong flavour. It burns at relatively low temperatures.

shanghai noodles These fresh, white wheat-based noodles are commonly used in northern-style Chinese cooking. Store in the refrigerator.

shaoxing rice wine This aromatic liquid is made from fermented rice. Most of the best quality, more delicate flavoured brands come from Shaoxing.

shiitake mushrooms These are sold fresh and dried. The more pungent dried mushroom needs to be first rehydrated in hot water. Similar to Chinese dried mushrooms.

shimmering point Oil is ideal for frying at 190°C–200°C (375°F–400°F).

When the oil reaches this temperature, the surface of the oil will begin to shimmer or ripple.

sichuan peppercorns This pinkish brown, peppercorn-shaped spice is actually not a pepper but a berry from the prickly ash tree. Widely used in Chinese cooking, producing more of a numbing effect rather than being spicy or hot. Along with salt, it is the essential ingredient in sichuan salt and pepper mixture.

smoking point When oil reaches a certain temperature, about 210°C (415°F), it begins to smoke. This is the ideal temperature for frying some foods, or for heating oils.

soy chickens These chickens, braised in soy sauce, are sold in the speciality Chinese barbecue shops, which sell char siu (barbecued pork) and Peking ducks.

soy sauce Light soy sauce, often referred to simply as soy sauce, is a salty, brown sauce made from fermented soya beans. It is used as a seasoning in stir-fries, soups and dipping sauces. Dark soy sauce has molasses and sugar added, giving it a malty, rich flavour. Ideal for use in braises and slow-cooked dishes. Dark soy sauce is less salty than light soy sauce. Lee Kum Kee is a recommended brand.

soya beans These small yellow beans need soaking prior to cooking. They are also sold precooked in tins.

spring roll wrappers Thin, versatile pastry made with flour and water, used to wrap a filling before deep-frying. Store in the freezer.

star anise Similar to aniseed and liquorice, this star-shaped, intensely aromatic seed of the anise bush is used in soups and braises and is one of the flavours of five-spice. Star anise is also available ready ground.

stir-frying Stir-frying cooks food evenly and quickly, retaining its colour and texture. During stir-frying, the side of a wok maintains the heat. So, when adding liquid ingredients, do so by pouring the liquid down the side of the wok.

tapioca flour White and waxy-textured flour made from finely ground cassava root. Used to dust or coat food before frying.

tofu Tofu, or bean curd, is solidified soya milk. Silken (soft) tofu is smooth and delicate; silken firm is slightly more set; and firm or hard tofu is ideal for stir-frying or deep-frying. Fermented tofu is red to brown in colour, the result of the addition of mould. It has a strong, almost cheesy flavour and is best used in small amounts.

white peppercorns Native to India and used widely throughout Asia. They have a less intense heat than black peppercorns and their colour provides good contrast to braised and fried foods. Use freshly ground whenever possible.

won ton wrappers Either egg or wheat based, these pastries are used to wrap fillings before being steamed, fried or boiled.

yellow rock sugar Golden, crystal nuggets, which are a combination of white and brown sugar and honey. Not as sweet as white sugar, rock sugar makes an excellent toffee. An effective way to crush it, if required, is using a mortar and pestle. Smaller pieces will dissolve when cooked with liquid ingredients.

index

A

almond cookies, 180

B

bamboo shoots, 188
barbecued duck won tons
    with choy sum, 138
barley and vegetable soup, 24
beans
    beef and black bean casserole, 48
    black bean and chilli chicken with
        leeks, 60
    chinatown chicken casserole, 51
    fish with black beans and ginger, 56
beef
    beef and black bean casserole, 48
    chinatown carpaccio, 19
    honey beef in peking pancakes,
        148
    peppered beef and shiitake with
        rice noodles, 88
biscuits
    almond cookies, 180
    orange, almond and fennel seed
        biscuits, 179
black bean and chilli chicken with
    leeks, 60
black vinegar, 188

C

carpaccio, 19
cashew and chilli fried rice, 72
char kway teow, 95
char siu rack of lamb, 152
chicken
    black bean and chilli chicken
        with leeks, 60
    chinatown chicken casserole, 51
    chinatown chicken salad, 137
    gunpowder chicken, 104
    hoisin chicken, 111
    lemon chicken, 133

soy chicken with rice noodles and
    garlic chives, 55
soy roast chicken with ginger and
    spring onion, 59
spiced chicken salad, 92
spicy chicken in lettuce cups, 64
stock, 187, 188
velveted chicken with cashews and
    smoky chilli, 87
chicken stock, 187, 188
chilli
    black bean and chilli chicken
        with leeks, 60
    cashew and chilli fried rice, 72
    chilli blue swimmer crab, 96
    salt and chilli lobster, 39
    salt and chilli prawns, 67
    salt and chilli sweet corn, 76
    seared kingfish with orange and
        chilli oil, 91
    silken tofu with soy, chilli and
        spring onion, 36
    steamed salmon with chilli oil, 99
    velveted chicken with cashews
        and smoky chilli, 87
chilli sauce, 188
chilli–garlic sauce, 188
chillies, dried, 188
chinatown carpaccio, 19
chinatown chicken casserole, 51
chinatown chicken salad, 137
chinatown mushroom and tofu
    stir-fry, 40
chinatown osso bucco with orange, 155
chinatown pilau, 100
chinatown salsa with won ton
    crisps, 118
chinatown toffeed figs, 167
cinnamon sticks, 188
combination omelette, 52
crumbed prawns with citrus dip, 117
cumin lamb skewers, 71

D

desserts
    chinatown toffeed figs, 167
    five-spiced plumcots, 175
    fried ice cream with butterscotch
        sauce, 168
    fruit salad with spiced lime
        syrup, 176
    jasmine tea ice cream, 172
    mandarin sorbet, 171
dry-roasting, 188
duck
    barbecued duck won tons with
        choy sum, 138
    duck with rice noodles and bamboo
        shoots, 47
    duck spring rolls with orange
        anise dip, 144
    duck and star anise broth with
        shanghai noodles, 79
    mandarin and sweet spiced
        duck, 159
    soy and spice braised duck, 107

E

eggplant
    eggplant, cumin and black bean
        salad, 108
    eggplant in special sauce, 164
    steamed eggplant with vinegar
        and garlic, 134
eggs
    combination omelette, 52
    egg noodles, 188
    egg rolls with vegetables and
        coriander, 15

F

figs, toffeed, 167
fish with black beans and ginger, 56
five-spice, 188
five-spiced plumcots, 175

fried ice cream with butterscotch
  sauce, 168
fruit salad with spiced lime syrup, 176

G
garlic spareribs, 23
ginger broth with barbecued pork, 16
ground bean sauce, 188
gunpowder chicken, 104

H
hoisin chicken, 111
hoisin sauce, 188
honey beef in peking pancakes, 148
honey prawns, 151
hot and sour mushroom soup, 126

I
ice cream
  fried ice cream with butterscotch
    sauce, 168
  jasmine tea ice cream, 172

K
kingfish, seared, with orange and
  chilli oil, 91

L
lamb
  char siu rack of lamb, 152
  cumin lamb skewers, 71
  roast lamb with cumin and black
    vinegar, 84
lap cheong sausages, 95, 188
lemon chicken, 133
lobster, salt and chilli, 39
lychee delight, 184

M
mandarin sorbet, 171
mandarin and sweet spiced duck, 159
mum's ginger and almond slice, 183

mushroom soy sauce, 188
mushrooms
  chinatown mushroom and tofu
    stir-fry, 40
  hot and sour mushroom soup, 126
  peppered beef and shiitake with rice
    noodles, 88
  shiitake and gai larn stir-fry, 32

N
noodles
  char kway teow, 95
  duck with rice noodles and bamboo
    shoots, 47
  duck and star anise broth with
    shanghai noodles, 79
  peppered beef and shiitake with rice
    noodles, 88
  rice stick noodles with seafood, 43
  sesame noodles with garlic chives, 28
  soy chicken with rice noodles and
    garlic chives, 55
  steamed prawns with tangy spinach
    noodles, 122

O
omelette; combination, 52
orange, almond and fennel seed
  biscuits, 179
oyster sauce, 188
oysters with rice vinegar and salmon
  roe, 114

P
pepper and salt mixture, sichuan, 189
peppered beef and shiitake with rice
  noodles, 88
pickles, 188
pork
  char kway teow, 95
  garlic spareribs, 23
  ginger broth with barbecued pork, 16

pork with orange and sweet
    pickles, 163
  roasted pork loin with fennel and soy,
    80
  sweet and sour pork, 156
potatoes
  salt and pepper potatoes, 75
  stir-fried potato with black vinegar, 31
prawns
  combination omelette, 52
  crumbed prawns with citrus dip, 117
  honey prawns, 151
  prawn, celery and garlic fried rice, 35
  prawns with ginger and spring onion,
    20
  salt and chilli prawns, 67
  steamed prawns with garlic soy, 12
  steamed prawns with tangy spinach
    noodles, 122

R
rice
  cashew and chilli fried rice, 72
  chinatown pilau, 100
  prawn, celery and garlic fried rice, 35
rice noodles, 189
rice stick noodles, 189
  with seafood, 43
roast lamb with cumin and black vinegar,
  84
roasted pork loin with fennel and soy, 80

S
salads
  chinatown chicken salad, 137
  eggplant, cumin and black bean salad,
    108
  spiced chicken salad, 92
  tomato and coriander salad, 129
salmon
  salmon won tons with ginger and
    red vinegar dip, 121

steamed, with chilli oil, 99
sweet soy-glazed salmon, 160
salsa, chinatown salsa with won ton
crisps, 118
salt and chilli lobster, 39
salt and chilli prawns, 67
salt and chilli sweet corn, 76
salt and pepper potatoes, 75
salt and pepper tofu, 83
salt and pepper trout with cucumber
salad, 103
salted black beans, 189
seafood
chilli blue swimmer crab, 96
crumbed prawns with citrus dip, 117
fish with black beans and ginger, 56
honey prawns, 151
oysters with rice vinegar and salmon
roe, 114
prawn, celery and garlic fried rice, 35
prawns with ginger and spring onion,
20
rice stick noodles with seafood, 43
salmon won tons with ginger and red
vinegar dip, 121
salt and chilli lobster, 39
salt and chilli prawns, 67
salt and pepper trout with cucumber
salad, 103
seared kingfish with orange and chilli
oil, 91
steamed prawns with garlic soy, 12
steamed prawns with tangy spinach
noodles, 122
steamed salmon with chilli oil, 99
sugar and soy cured tuna, 147
sweet and sour fish, 141
sweet soy-glazed salmon, 160
trout with stir-fried almonds and
celery, 44
tuna spring rolls with sweet and sour
sauce, 125

seared kingfish with orange and
chilli oil, 91
sesame noodles with garlic chives, 28
shanghai noodles, 189
shaoxing rice wine, 189
shiitake and gai larn stir-fry, 32
shiitake mushrooms, 189
sichuan pepper and salt mixture, 187
sichuan peppercorns, 189
silken tofu with soy, chilli and spring
onion, 36
soup
barley and vegetable, 24
duck and star anise broth with
shanghai noodles, 79
ginger broth with barbecued pork, 16
hot and sour mushroom, 126
tomato eggflower soup, 68
soy chicken with rice noodles and garlic
chives, 55
soy roast chicken with ginger and spring
onion, 59
soy sauce, 189
soy and spice braised duck, 107
spiced chicken salad, 92
spicy chicken in lettuce cups, 64
spring roll wrappers, 189
spring rolls
duck, with orange anise dip, 144
tuna, with sweet and sour sauce,
125
star anise, 189
steamed eggplant with vinegar and
garlic, 134
steamed prawns with garlic soy, 12
steamed prawns with tangy spinach
noodles, 122
steamed salmon with chilli oil, 99
stir-fried potato with black vinegar, 31
stir-fry of garlic chives, capsicum and
coriander, 130
sugar and soy cured tuna, 147

sweet and sour fish, 141
sweet and sour pork, 156
sweet soy-glazed salmon, 160

T
tofu, 189
chinatown mushroom and tofu stir-fry,
40
salt and pepper tofu, 83
silken tofu with soy, chilli and spring
onion, 36
tofu with soy and ginger, 27
tomato and coriander salad, 129
tomato eggflower soup, 68
tuna
spring rolls with sweet and sour sauce,
125
sugar and soy cured, 147

V
vegetables
eggplant, cumin and black bean salad,
108
eggplant in special sauce, 164
salt and chilli sweet corn, 76
shiitake and gai larn stir-fry, 32
steamed eggplant with vinegar and
garlic, 134
stir-fry of garlic chives, capsicum and
coriander, 130
velveted chicken with cashews and smoky
chilli, 87

W
won ton wrappers, 189
won tons
barbecued duck, with choy sum, 138
salmon, with ginger and red vinegar
dip, 121

Y
yellow rock sugar, 189